YOU WANT BLOOD?

YOU WANT THUNDER?

YOU WANT GUTSY GUITAR?

You can get it inside this year's bloodiest rock book!

Rock's arcane heavies have been getting their blood up for long enough and they're now ready to give you their side of the story. Kiss by Robert Duncan tells it in their own words. It tells it in the words of those who have seen them get their blood together from their earliest days and watched them rock their way to superstardom. It tells it in the words of their bloody fans, their critics, their mockers and their worshippers.

Kiss gives you the low down on the band who rose out of Brooklyn, Queens and the Bronx to stamp a new style of heavy rock'n'roll on a world gone soft at the poles.

Dare you read the Savoy Kiss of Death?

Then read on . . .

ROBERT DUNCAN

SAVOY BOOKS
A Savoy Rock'n'Roll Book

In Association with
NEW ENGLISH LIBRARY
TIMES MIRROR

Copyright 1978, 1980 by Robert Duncan

Published by Savoy Books Ltd, 279 Deansgate, Manchester
M3 4EW, England.

Epigraph from "Send in the Clowns" — music and lyrics by
Stephen Sondheim, copyright 1973. All rights reserved.

Editorial consultant, Savoy edition: Ace of Manchester

ISBN 0 86130 040 8

Printed by S.E.T. Limited, Manchester, England

For Roni Hoffman
and
Rusty Duncan III,
the fans

"Send in the clowns . . .
Don't bother, they're here."

Stephen Sondheim

KISS—The Book: Contents

DEBITS & CREDITS

Writing an Unauthorized Biography, Beatles Obituary, and New Age Rock 'n' Roll Saga has to be about the most difficult thing I have done since quitting Sky King for playing too much Jethro Tull. Fortunately, I don't carry grudges (Phil Leone, come home). In any case, a lot of thanks are due to the following people, without whom . . . well . . . without whom:

Richard Robinson, for telling me I *should*, at the Black Sabbath party, and then making it possible.

Ed Ward, for getting me started (thanks, I think).

John Morthland, for my first job; Dave Marsh, for suggesting it to me.

Lester Bangs, for writing great and Bolos; Air-Wreck Genheimer, for the Disco-On-Wheels of Life; Charlie, for Halsted; *Creem*, in general (Harvey, Barracks, Siegel, Connie, Jann, *et al.*), for a place to do it.

Sue Whitall, for Number-One Kiss Army Re-searchingness and pals.

Kevin Doyle, for always coming through with laughs, food, Citicash, habitat, and drinks (drinks!).

Ned Alexander, for much the same with two dollars in the mouth.

The Shark, for laughs, habitat, *The Godfather*, and Robert DeNiro; not forgetting Chris, for the postcard, and Woj, for the hospital visit.

St. David's, St. David's . . .

Jeremy Koch, for getting it there (Kitty for getting him there).

Tom "Ro" Rose, for the grits, the car, and the Belmont.

Parky Conyngham for fresh dairy, mirrors, and the Deck (RIP).

Sam Rorick, for the funniest laughs (in clay, too!), hat jelly, and peyote visions (thanks, Nick).

Fair Kissies we . . .

Billy Altman, for title quotes, Swamp Fox, and the last word on rock 'n' roll (thanks, Mugs).

The Bells of Hell (Peter, David, Barry, Barbara, Barbara's mother, Lee, Beau, Nick, no rock crits, *et al.*), for (drinks!).

Femi Omole, for Total Unmitigated Kindness and lousy sandwiches.

Pasquale's (Molly, Wanda, the Blond Bombshell, *et al.*), for not tossing us out.

Pete and Randy Levin, for my first story; Ed DonDiego, for Elvis; Jumpin' Jack Fiorillo, for James Joyce.

Lance Duncan, for the best damn guitarist in the future western world.

Rusty and Diana Duncan, my favorite sailor and his gal in the only port, for love, inspiration, and granite guts.

Joanie and Ben Case for love, harassment, and military competence.

Dana Duncan (Little Rusty: see front), Thomas, Joanne, and Jennifer Case, for the future.

Roy and Sarah Hoffman, for the girl.

Mimi and Russ Duncan, for the works.

And: Southside Johnny, the Disrespectful Too, for the Jukes Forever.

Plus: Mike Kaplan and Typing, etc. for twenty percent; Irene Tumulty for ten percent; and Kate Duffy for the rest. All photos by the intrepid Michael N. Marks/Creem. Patient photo editor: Roni Hoffman/Veronica Drew Ink.

Lastly, interminable credit and profuse thanks are due to Flying Puppy Airlines from their one and only grateful passenger, for no turbulence and service above and beyond.

Hey, guys: Is this what you want???

Robert Duncan
Gum Joy, New York
August 1, 1977

SIDE ONE

Chapter 1
The Midnight Sun

We started to do this because we believed in it
—not because it was a joke.

Paul Stanley, October 1976

June, 1976. It is the end of a perfect summer's day. There is not a cloud in the sky, and a gentle breeze is coaxing twilight across verdant New Jersey meadows.

The end of a perfect summer's day: when twilight heralds a darkness that, no matter how crisp and clear, is all the more unnerving, all the more death-confirming for the starkness of the contrast. *What will happen tomorrow? Will it rain and thunder? Will it merely threaten to do so? Will the ghastly lightning strike my house then? Or will the sun beam down again in all its munificent, autocratic glory? Will I be happy or sad? Will I even* live *tomorrow?*

Night, at these times, brings no comfort. Night for now is the end of joy, the time when the world closes its eyes and flails out at the smallness, the aloneness, the hopelessness. Night here, now, is the time when some swill spirits, some toke the herb, some pop pills, and some go so insane they do not need to.

The end of a perfect summer's day—and much more, to be sure.

Night has wrapped itself languorously about the aging rafters of New Jersey's Roosevelt Stadium. It is ten o'clock, and there is no mistaking, at this point: Night is here to stay.

Fifteen thousand human souls crowd the stadium structure, high into the reaches of its upper level, and below spill out to fill the infield, psychically huddled, physically flailing—against the night. Flailing, as in the weird and wild and wondrously relieving movements of rock 'n' roll.

Roosevelt Stadium has become a place—briefly—of rock 'n' roll, the life-style with the crushing backbeat.

Roosevelt used to be a place where they played football and baseball and the crowds came to cheer on the Republic, her hot dogs, her beer, and her lithe bodies. Her daylight. A place they came to celebrate their freedom, their boundless energy, and to show off their enthusiasm. Roosevelt is a monument to happy things that are now old. They are that way—old—because some people heard the blues and saw the night and then some others took action. They began to lash out and thunder and scream. They began to pound. They raised their voices in a high-holy electric caterwaul and clawed at the lining of heaven: Some began to play rock 'n' roll.

Now, in 1976, high atop a floodlit platform in old Roosevelt Stadium, they are continuing to play rock 'n' roll, while on the infield and on into the farthest heights of the tiers the fifteen thousand flail and churn in mad rock 'n' roll time.

Mad rock 'n' roll time. Bob Seger has played it this day, hard. Point Blank has played it this day, harder. And, as twilight approached, J. Geils has twisted it and teased it and then sprung it to let it wail. Mad rock 'n' roll time. Three bands have played this day in mad rock 'n' roll time. And then came night, and then there is a lull.

There is a lull now, as the full impact of the night settles in. There is a lull now, at ten o'clock, while other things begin to happen in the low light of the stage where the spotlights now go dim. There is a lull. Night clamps tight on Roosevelt Stadium and shadowy forms dart quickly on the stage. A lull. Right at this very moment, at ten o'clock, there is a calm. There is a calm, just as there ought to be, just as they told us there would be, and just as there always is . . .

Because then there is a storm!

An explosion onstage, and fifteen thousand are blinded at one fell swoop. An explosion onstage—Sweet Jesus! An unholy shattering of the night. A split-second vanquishment of one holy terror for another! The end of a perfect day, indeed!

And in an alphabet twelve feet high, suspended above the stage, shimmering with the reflected light of the blast like the technological age's answer to the Burning Bush, stands one word: *KISS*. "KISS," read the fifteen thousand. And as the visual din subsides and eyes adjust to the new light (and the New Light) now emanating from the stage, the aural din begins.

The rock group *Kiss* has taken the stage.

The end of a perfect summer's day is the perfect end. And, as fifteen thousand young people know, the end to a whole lot else: baseball, football, and hey-get-your-cold-beer-here; the flag, the family, the Fonz, and Laverne and her stuck-up Shirley; Beethoven, Bach, Tchaikowsky, and Coltrane; Miles Davis and Miles Laboratories; Wall Street, Basin Street, Bleecker Street, and Bloomingdale's. The end goes on, and now the young minds teem with the possibilities: And maybe even rock 'n' roll? The death of rock 'n' roll . . . and then the Night? The end of the night, the beginning of the dawn, new light, new air, new *life* . . . Could it be? Could it be that they are bearing witness to the inexorable black dawn, the fertile Armageddon, the new music, the new reaction, the new thrust forward?

Paul Stanley, alive with his star, screams into the mike: "Good evening, Jersey City!" And the band is off with "Deuce."

Yes! thinks the crowd as the bass rumbles in their bowels, the drums pound back to unseen cavemen, guitars twist and burn, and Stanley belts forth the song from eons beneath his heart. *Yes!* they think. And it is energizing and completely frightening at the same time. *Yes!* As flames fly and lights swoop, and in chrome and leather, the band stands up to its own sweet holocaust of quarter-notes. *Yes!* This is nothing less than doom's thundering peace. And Kiss is the conquering demi-legion of the Night, the bearer of the New Age. The New Age of Fire.

The four members of the band—Paul Stanley, Gene Simmons, Ace Frehley, and Peter Criss—in costume (or is that their real *skin?*) stand close to seven feet tall. Their black-and-silver costume/

skins variously transform them into reptile, space-man, diamond-studded puppy dog (the Diamond Dog, perhaps, of David Bowie's song/fantasy?), and alley cat. All of which is nearly mundane when the gaze falls upon their faces, those unlike any other faces. The faces of Kiss, corresponding to the bodies of Kiss—that is, to their costume/skins—are the faces of a cat, a starry-eyed pup, a bat-lizard, and a person from another galaxy. Some say the black, white, and silver faces of the members of Kiss are evil incarnate. Some of the people who say this come readily, others are drawn against their will. For whatever one says about the faces and the costumes they wrap around their beings, there is no way one can resist looking and looking and looking again.

When all this physical presence is placed in the context of the Kiss stage show, one can only become weak.

Explosion? Well, it's more than just a physical detonation on a stage. It's more than just sixteen flashpots ignited simultaneously across and around a stage. The moment the stage spotlights dim completely, the moment before all is relit in the blinding flash-powder detonation is one of the most delicious moments one can ever experience.

It's not the kind of thing that happens before Crosby, Stills & Nash come out on stage. It's not the same as when they dim the lights before Aerosmith comes out on stage. Not the same as the seconds before Neil Diamond or Carole King or Queen or Fleetwood Mac or Peter Frampton or the Stones or ZZ Top or the Wailers come out on stage. The moment before Kiss comes on stage is most nearly akin to the moment before your very first girl friend slips the very first strap from her shoulder for the first time. It's a moment that is so tentative and so certain at the same time, so vivid and so blurred, so eagerly anticipated and so reluctantly approached, that it is over before it began, and invariably looms as the dominant mood of the evening as it fades into memory.

It may be that the anticipation of Kiss is better than the anticipation of first sex.

That the time spent driving in from Philly and Hartford and Rye and Dayton to see a concert in Jersey City's Roosevelt Stadium creates a more intense anticipation for Kiss than years of looking at dirty magazines creates for the sexual experience.

Some might say, at this admittedly extreme point: "You gotta be a fan, I guess." The point is: *But you don't.* Come to a Kiss concert and see what I mean.

In other words, the explosion that happens when Kiss appears on stage is an explosion in the heart, the mind, the soul, the groin, whatever you want to call it, of every one of the fifteen thousand assembled in this stadium tonight.

By the time one can think, Ace Frehley is marching down from his turret emplacement at the rear of the Gothic stage set for the solo in "Strutter." "Strutter" is about a nasty girl, and no one is as nasty as Ace when he stomps down from his spot ten feet above the stage in his rolled silver naugahyde boots, wielding his Les Paul to express his musical disdain for the Strutter. As usual, Ace never looks into the faces of the crowd below him,

preferring to stare off, grimacing, into some inter-
planetary space that lies somewhere along a
tangent that might be drawn to the trajectory of a
home-run ball hit over the left-field fence. The
Left-Field Planet—that must be where Ace is from.
That Strutter girl could not be farther beneath him.

All—except for the Kitty Kat, the alley denizen—they are all stage-front now, wrangling with
some of the loudest music ever exhibited before
humans, coaxing the audience ever onward into
the sonic oblivion. "Nothin' To Lose" . . . and
Paul is skidding over to stage-right to wag heads
with Ace, as Gene tells the audience what's what—
that they "got nothin' to lose." Bat-Lizard Simmons
is faced front-and-center to the audience, his eerie
bat-wing eyes staring them down as his Long Pink
whips out periodically, taunting. The little chore-
ography of Stanley and Frehley to his left, the
simultaneous shaking of the hair and bobbing of
the bodies, is almost a grotesque and menacing
parody of the steps and hair antics of the Beatles,
and other lesser Merseyside groups such as Gerry
and the Pacemakers. The dance steps work as
parody, and they work in their own right, serving
to highlight Simmons.

But it's only the beginning.

Sixteen hundred pounds of flash powder later;
beyond the flashing red lights and Paul's camping
around with the fireman's hat in "Firehouse"; after Ace and Gene have traveled up and down their
respective turrets several more times; after the
strobes have strobed and the eyes of the mastiffs
that guard Peter's platform have lit horribly; after
Gene has breathed real and true fire from deep in

his hot soul—all that while later, past all that information that is too much to absorb, comes the climax. It's a climax that serves to focus the audience on the deepest and darkest core, the blackhole center, of Kiss.

It is a climax that focuses on and through and mercifully back out from the mind of Gene Simmons.

There is a bass solo in "Rock Bottom." Simmons steps to the edge of the stage, grinding. His shoes, the audience can see, are actually the faces of angry silver gargoyles whose red eyes bug out, not unlike those of Simmons himself beneath his batwing eyebrows. Gene is leering at the crowd beneath him. As if to hurt, perhaps.

More likely, as if to violate *in toto*.

Suddenly the tongue—the longest any of them have ever seen—begins to unfurl from his mouth and slither down his chin as he falls into a hideous squatting position, the silver of his black-leather and metallic codpiece winking light lasciviously out at those who can still look. He is leaning this way, from his squat, and then the other way, all the time the tongue lapping at the air, the eyes bugging, the eyes on the *shoes* bugging, the crotch winking. In a moment, the line between sex and violence becomes blurred—for real.

What does this Bat-Lizard want? What does he intend?

His fingers run up and down the fretboard of the bass, the black danglies attached to his gauntlet gloves working furiously in some contradictory direction.

And then there is blood.

Blood pouring all over the stage from the impenetrable void behind the black lips of the bat creature. Suddenly, his sex *is* violence—and vice-versa. Puddles of the discharge form on the stage beneath his face, and a bloody trail obscures his white chin. Sometimes the blood from his mouth splashes across the front rows.

And the madman leers.

Is he sick? Is he dying? Is he regurgitating some horrible dinner that is beyond the comprehension of civilized humankind?

And just as precipitously as his carnage has begun, it is over, and Ace and Paul and Peter are back in their places on the stage and the entire unit of destruction/redemption roars gloriously into the metal-thunder finale of "Rock Bottom."

The squeamish have lost lunch.

Is violence sex? Is sex violence? What are we to make of this modern world?

Or are we just afraid of the night?

Kiss is in triumph. The black shroud conquered, submissive—if not actually vanquished.

That the show continues, that there are more explosions, does not matter at this point. That they perform their incredible anthem, their rallying cry (and what may perhaps be the rallying cry of a generation) (*you* know . . .), that Peter Criss's drums rise twenty feet in the air, and every time he hits the cymbals, lights pop and sizzle, almost does not matter. All of that is almost showbiz, put up against the bloody tongue of Gene Simmons.

The fact that much of the audience is drunk or drugged out or hysterical or comatose from the proceedings barely matters.

It's the tongue.

The tongue is saying it all. The tongue is speaking for posterity. It's this bloody tongue that derides the baseball and the football and the beer and the bluesmen and the jazzmen and all things surrounding them. It's that damnable and repulsive bloody tongue.

Not the hysterical, drunken, and/or drugged-up ravings. Not the terror of the firecracker wads. Not the trampling and the dying. Not the pretty young girl with the tiny gold necklace who is comatose and lies by the back gate, completely unaware that she is awaiting an ambulance. None of that.

It's the tongue.

And, here in the late 1970s, it is the climax of the show—no, the climax of an era: an horrifically extended crimson tongue spills chicken blood down through the ages—which is just about how long it's been—onto a skinny little greaseball with wiggly hips who thinks he ain't nothin' but a hound dog. He's dead and gone to fat, the grotesque dribblings of the tongue tell us. Hope I die before I get old, they used to say. Done, even forgotten, says the red dribble-dribble. Billion Dollar Babies become Billion Dollar Old Men: Go away, it says. Down through the ages, all over those ages, the tongue drips its sloppy substance without mercy . . . till the ages are where they're supposed to be: Back There. Old. Decrepit. And, worst of all, wavering. Goodbye, Elvis. Goodbye, Rolling Stones. Goodbye, Pete Townshend. Good riddance, Alice Cooper. The Kings are dead. The crimson tongue demands:

OY WANNA ROK UN ROWL AWL NOYT UN PAWDY EV-VARY DEH!!!

A stadium in America cheers and blows some brains out.

The following means more to some people living in this decade than does any religion, job, emotional involvement, or even their own name: *Kiss*.

And if that sounds a little like John Lennon's famous statement of 1966 regarding his band, the Beatles—"We're more popular than Jesus."—well, the effect is not altogether unintentional on my part—or on the part of Kiss.

The members of the rock group Kiss are part of a generation that is a semi-cohesive unit because we're all children of the Beatles. Perhaps even more than by television, this generation, which is now between twenty-three and thirty years old, has been nurtured by the music, the lyrics, the movies, the public pronouncements and activities (and the rumors about the private activities) of the four moptops.

Nutured thusly, the generation also became defined by the Beatles. When they grew *their* hair, we grew ours. When *they* dropped acid, *we* dropped acid. When *they* knocked organized religion, *we* knocked it too. And, ultimately, when *they* broke up (in 1970, to all intents and purposes) so did our generation, fragmenting to individual pursuits—some cutting their hair, some leaving it long, some continuing further into the drug world, some retreating, some taking up with jazz, some with folk, some with classical music, some staying with rock.

But all that aside, perhaps the single most important facet of the Beatles' remarkable influence on a generation has been our conception of the scope of our lives. The Beatles blew out all the old realities. The old parameters, the old possibilities went out the window. They showed us the possibility of incredible wealth, seemingly limitless adulation. In essence: the ability to have power. Anybody, it was presumed, could be a Beatle, a modern monarch-without-portfolio; anybody could have vast power. To a teen-ager, that has a singular appeal. If, in 1964, he wasn't a football player, that was it—in terms of adulation, in terms of commanding people. And here he was, his face breaking out all over the place, his pants busting out all over the place, everybody from his teachers to the girl next door on the defensive line is down on him. How is he to get back? He wants to show them! Then, *voila*: the Beatles. Attractive? Perhaps more than some. Talented? Possibly—but after all it's *only* rock 'n' roll. At the core of the matter, the Beatles were simply Everyman.

So millions of fat, pimply teen-agers started forming bands—to show 'em! And some of these teen-agers lived in the outer boroughs of New York City.

Paul Stanley was always fat, still has a tendency to it. Gene Simmons, while tall and not overweight, was nonetheless no prize. Peter Criss, who had always considered a career in music, was just a little bit older—and maybe a little too short. Ace

Frehley was just plain angry—a rebuilt cheekbone attests to his pugnacious nature as a teen. All in all, these four kids from the "outer boroughs"—Brooklyn, the Bronx, and Queens, places sophisticated Manhattanites will barely acknowledge—were perfect fodder for the Dream Machine that the Beatles fostered. And, in the mid-sixties—to turn around John Lennon's later, more apocalyptic statement: The dream had just begun.

It would be over a decade before the dream would be realized by these four boys, before Gene Simmons, the demon Bat-Lizard of Kiss, would fling his tongue out to drip his crimson disdain for the ages down on the old heroes. But some never doubted for a second that the dream would come true.

Chapter 2
Primeval Oozings

I think car crashes are neat—but you can't tap
your foot to them . . .
                              Gene Simmons, October 1976

So the Beatles were the fulcrum for a generation—still, there was a lot that led from the hal-
cyon days of Beatlemania in 1964 to the
emergence of Kiss in late 1973, a lot which is important to the true tale of *the* phenomenon of our
times.

To return briefly to ancient history: The
Beatles—no matter what others will have you
know—begat the Rolling Stones. Without the
success of the Beatles—who were viewed as fairly
clean-cut, decent boys by most adults—a group that
absolutely and manifestly flew in the face of everything that was wholesome would have been unnecessary. Without the Beatles in the number-one
slot on the pop charts there would have been no
need for a group—it turned out to be the Rolling

Stones—to challenge them on their own ball field and form a diametrically opposite (so we were hyped to believe) aesthetic and moral position. (If the truth be known, to those of us who were reveling in the sweet harmonies and crashingly honest "Yeah, yeah, yeah"s of the Beatles, the Rolling Stones *did* seem rude, undisciplined, immoral—and, of course, *completely* alluring.)

So, Beatles to Rolling Stones. This opened up a whole 'nother end of the spectrum. Enter: Eric Burdon and the Animals, and the Yardbirds. The Animals were sleazier than the Stones—demonstrably uglier, for sure—and the Yardbirds were louder and played with more sophistication (ironically) but with no less insanity. At which point, you have these components to the rock scene: Extraordinary Popularity, Sleaziness, Lack of Discipline, and Loudness and Technical Adequacy. (I admit to ignoring many of the less germane British Invasion bands.)

Before long it's 1967 and the Summer of Love and Hippies, and you get the Mothers of Invention wearing dresses and *everybody* wearing psychedelic makeup. Acid is entrenched (see the Grateful Dead, Jefferson Airplane). At the same time, gender confusion is just starting up.

It's 1968 and, in Arizona, Vincent Furnier and his band the Spiders are looking for any way to make a splash (which was the nature of the times). In Detroit, in 1969, they hit on it! They dub themselves Alice Cooper, put on slinky feminine clothing and makeup, and appear on their first album cover (for Frank Zappa's Straight label) as the first androgynes of rock. It was rumored over the next several years that Alice, as the lead singer became dubbed, cut off chicken's heads onstage. What is certain is that he beheaded plastic baby dolls and mugged Santa Claus. And thusly was the Shocking Rock of the Rolling Stones taken just three steps forward.

In New York City, naturally, Alice Cooper was not taken lightly. In fact, bands like Teenage Lust, the Harlots of 42nd Street, and the New York Dolls seemed to dedicate their careers to doing him one better. The fact that none of these bands could play their instruments or sing any better than Alice's band or the legendary Stooges didn't matter apparently. Club owners who demanded Top-40 songs be damned: They would find their own venues. Their original venue became the Mercer Arts Center on the southeast outskirts of Greenwich Village. If they couldn't play a dance tune in a club—well, of course, they must be artists. Soon inept but outrageous bands were flocking to the Mercer—and, somewhat later, to Max's Kansas City, uptown on Park Avenue—with tapes.

In the meantime, somebody decided to revive the ballroom of the seedy Diplomat Hotel on West 46th Street as a place for live entertainment, of the rock variety naturally. While it had been a lovely room to dance in in the forties, and had briefly served as a psychedelic outpost in the Summer of Love, little else had been thought of for the Diplomat. Everyone assumed that like all the other seedy Times Square hotels it would go to the junkies, the pimps, and the prosties, and from there to demolition. Gene Simmons and Paul Stanley had the idea of booking the ballroom at the Dip, and several months later, Kiss made their *official* Manhattan debut there in the summer of 1973. But I'm ahead of myself.

Press coverage of the Mercer Arts scene boomed, beginning with the *Village Voice*, later slipping over onto the pages of the rock magazines, like *Rolling Stone* and *Creem*, and even into the hallowed columns of the *New York Times*. Bolstered by the generally positive, consistently hot press, the Mercer Arts Center thrived on the crowds swelling its snaky passageways and cavelike atmosphere, and the bands thrived right along with it. Nobody was getting rich off the venture, but for these guys who couldn't play the traditional clubs in the area—due to temperament or ineptitude or a winning combination of both—the scam was working.

So if you accept the axiom that everybody and his mongoloid brother started playing guitar in the wake of the Beatles, and that half of these nascent musicians finally bloomed into something akin to full-fledged rock 'n' rollers, then you know that there were lots of competent and lots more incompetent bands looking for a place to ply their trade. Now—as might be expected—the "in" groups at the Mercer were trying their best to maintain the venue as a closed circuit. In other words, they wanted the gigs to rotate among themselves, the select few earlybirds—Teenage Lust, the Dolls, the Harlots; as soon as they'd found a sucker, they weren't going to let him go. Suffice it to say that it got pretty damned hard to get a job at the Mercer after the hype exploded. Which probably spared us all a lot of sonic grief.

However, Paul Stanley and Gene Simmons would not be swayed from their appointed stairway to stardom. Toward such heavenly realms, they acquired a loft near Twenty-third Street and Fifth Avenue, right around the corner from the Manhattan Toy Center (another place where they make things for kids). Here they would rehearse and audition players and, as Simmons told me, "get it right!" These guys were not just your average Beatles-inspired Alice Cooper-led space-outs; they meant business, and were, most importantly, willing to go about it in a businesslike, professional way. How they got this way has a lot to do with how they got the loft.

As with much of, if you'll pardon the apt expression, Kisstory, the saga of the rock band Kiss—facts, figures, names, and dates are cloudy on this point. But even in the days before *New York* magazine rendered loft living de rigueur for the hip Manhattanite, you didn't get a loft for nothing. You had to have money. None of the band members' families are wealthy by any stretch, so it appears that Stanley and Simmons forked over their own dough for the practice pad. Where could it have come from? Well, Simmons worked as a copy assistant at *Vogue*, and Stanley worked the odd job . . . No, what emerges when one digs deep enough is that Simmons and Stanley (possibly under different names) were in a band that was signed to Columbia Records in the late Sixties or, the early Seventies; a band that cut one album which, for unknown reasons, never saw release. While the tapes of that recording presumably remain buried in the CBS vaults under the obscure

name of that hapless group, the band did allegedly
receive a sizable advance from the company for
signing back then. Apparently, this money is what
Gene and Paul invested in their new venture,
Kiss, in the form of rent for the loft. (Needless to
say, that early Simmons-Stanley collaboration is
one of the Great Lost Documents of our time. Undoubtedly, such an early recording will be worth a
small mint someday to the guy intrepid enough to
uncover it in the voluminous CBS stockpile! I
wonder, will it sound like Kiss? Or will it be revealed to us that Paul Stanley and Gene Simmons
once made Barry Manilow music—in other words,
kitsch, not Kiss!)

Which brings us around to the point: Stanley
and Simmons were more or less professionals when
they formed Kiss. They had been there once, and,
presumably, had learned some of the complicated
ropes of the music industry. They knew what others less experienced failed to recognize: that to
make it in music requires more than just talent,
that success in any area of show biz demands persistence. So where others banged their heads fruit-
lessly against the doors of the Mercer Arts Center
and then walked off defeated, Gene and Paul were
willing to make an end run around the whole over-
stuffed scene.

Teamed, of course, with Peter Criss, likewise a
veteran of several fairly unsuccessful recording
deals (the last with a band called Chelsea that
waxed perhaps as many as two LPs for Decca
Records), and the relative neophyte Ace Frehley,
Gene and Paul finally prevailed upon a nightclub
in Queens, New York, just outside Manhattan, to

present their very first gig as Kiss. As was evident
at the show on that first fateful evening, January
30, 1973, Kiss may have possessed that *sine qua
non* of music-biz success, persistence, but they had
yet to encompass several other ultimately significant elements. Most notably: a gimmick, *their*
gimmick.

The makeup and the costumes were a little
rough.

But there's something you have to understand
before we travel back to that dark, smoky club
where the Kiss Era began. You have to understand
Queens. Because it's not just where the band made
its professional debut; it's also where they come
from. I don't mean literally—I mean in their souls.
And to hail from Queens in your soul is a state of
being that will always have a profound effect upon
your life.

Queens. Listen to the name of the place, the
word. Allow it to evoke an image in your brain,
and you're getting closer to understanding the
minds of the greatest rock 'n' roll band of all time.
Unlike Brooklyn, a word which puffs mightily
(that "city" also proclaims itself "the fourth largest
city in America"), or the Bronx, which snarls, or
Manhattan, which with all its syllables fairly looks
down its Empire State Building nose at you, the
word Queens whines in a most unappealing way. It
complains—but in a sniveling manner that ultimately
signals acceptance of the inferior status imposed
upon it. The borough of Queens is an outer borough to Manhattan's elite and glamorous central
status. It is a place that is construed as outside and,
hence, a place of and for outsiders.

For a specific visual reference, the credit film
run at the opening and close of *All in the Family*
shows a not atypical street in Queens where the
Bunkers' house is located. As you may see in the
film, Queens, while not being Manhattan (or
Bronx or Brooklyn), is not even sure it is Queens.
By which I mean, Queens is part suburb—many
of the homes have lawns—and part city—the lawns
are postage-stamp size and the houses are jammed
together like city dwellings. And it functions as
an ugly, compromised hybrid kin to both. Queens
also has freeways like Long Island, but traffic like
Manhattan. And then, of course, there are all those
factories and warehouses that make it look something like parts of Jersey City, of all things. In
short, Queens is a place where people are stuck.
And this idea that people are stuck in Queens,
and, to a lesser extent, in the other outer boroughs,
presents us with the idea of the Borough Mentality. Which is where, cleverly enough, the four
members of Kiss come in.

Each one is a child of a borough, of which
Queens is the archetypal, albeit most extreme, example. Each one was aware at one time of being
stuck and of being outside. And while the kids
starting up bands in Manhattan longed to be stars
just like their idols, the borough kids, the perennial outsiders, had to make a veritable quantum
leap to want anything so lofty—most would be satisfied to just be let "in." So the members of Kiss
had a double hunger at work within themselves:
They wanted "in," and then they wanted to go to
the top. This doubled hunger goes a long way
towards fostering the raw determination that kept

a band like Kiss going—pushing, cajoling, playing their asses off—until they got everything they wanted. While it's natural that Kiss avoided lower Manhattan's superhyped Mercer Arts scene and instead played their first gig at a club called the Coventry in Queens, it's also natural—natural selection *a la* Darwin, survival of the fittest, that is—that they, and not such Mercer darlings as Teenage Lust or the New York Dolls, eventually wound up playing Manhattan's loftiest venue, Madison Square Garden. The motivation, the guts it took to persist as others fell by the way, has a lot to do with Queens—and borough hunger.

But enough.

The Coventry is a nondescript (what else?) smoky little club in Queens where the owner decided he could draw more customers by presenting live rock 'n' roll. To a certain extent, he was taking a chance with Kiss because not only were they associated with the rather sloppy Mercer Arts—Max's Kansas City scene in Manhattan, but they were completely new. His instinctive feeling and somewhat courageous decision to book Kiss, however, panned out in spades. He drew crowds for Kiss, and everybody got along famously. As Gene put it to me once, referring to the early days at Coventry: "We've never played anywhere ever where we didn't get at least one encore!" Today, the club advertises as the place that discovered Kiss.

The Kiss act at the beginning was loud and bombastic, just as it is today. But where their stance in the current show might be construed as macho, back at the Coventry they were a lot more coquettish, affecting a version of the androgynous posturing that was popular at the time; their makeup was outrageous, but more in a mock-feminine direction as well. As one of them has said, "It wasn't really Kiss makeup. It was more feminine, like the Dolls." But the sum total of the Kiss show—as opposed to that of the Dolls, whom they so admired from afar—was still fantasy, escape, release. They never came on high-handed or contemptuously intellectual, as did some in the "in" scene. To the audience—the *Queens* audience, the outsiders—they were a sorely needed relief. Kiss provided a middle ground between the lofty artistes and the rote bar bands of the era. Kiss was a band they could really relate to.

Those early gigs in Queens were the harbinger of things to come. Kiss would succeed because they were willing to take in the majority, refusing to condescend. Kiss was—and is—a people's band, and that is one of the keys to their success.

On May 4, 1973, Kiss played their first Manhattan show in their rehearsal loft near the toy center. It was more a symbolic triumph over the Outer Borough syndrome than a substantive one. Nobody was getting rich and famous yet—but also nobody was faltering in conviction that someday such success would be theirs. The band played anywhere they could, in and around the city. When not playing, they rehearsed and held strategy meetings concerned with firming up their act and gaining the attention of the recording industry. During the course of these months of frantic and essentially unrewarded activity, the four band members came up with several ideas that were

such a combination of chutzpah and outright crazi-
ness that they could only be the product of genius—
the collective one of Kiss.

Unlike scores of other basement bands around
New York, Kiss finally figured out that they were
not skinny like the guys in the New York Dolls,
that, unlike the liver-lipped David Johanssen, none
of them would ever look sexy or even creepy-sexy
in a dress and eyeshadow. They would only look
like comedic imitations of the Dolls. "So," Frehley
has said matter-of-factly, "we decided to come on
real strong in black and silver." Genius idea number
one. The whiteface makeup in conjunction with
black leotards and imitation leather and chrome—
whatever they could scrounge up—was just the
touch that set them apart from the other makeup
bands, but not too far apart to be inaccessible: The
audience could follow the leap from female makeup
to theatrical paint.

Genius idea number two was that they decided
to become as proficient individually and as an ensemble on their instruments as they possibly could.
And if that sounds like an obvious idea, you don't
remember the Dolls or the Stooges from Detroit or
any of countless bands from around the country.
You don't know how bad they really were—even at
their best. Kiss knew that while people *might* respond to good *loose* music, it was a much better
bet that they would respond to good, *tight* music.

The clincher was genius idea number three:
The band also realized that the music business was
not built on staffs and clefs alone, but that to truly
make it, there had to be promotion. And while the
Dolls, who were wonderful but came and went in

about fifteen seconds, were charming the intellec-
tuals and disdaining promotion, Kiss put together
a mailing list of anyone they could think of in or
around music biz and began deluging their offices
with invites to gigs and promotional material.
Eventually, of course, they scored.

It happened at the Hotel Diplomat, and it happened under the auspices of another of the band's
bright ideas, which was: to rent the old ballroom
at the Dip when they couldn't get other gigs, and
produce their own shows. The Dip has a recent
history of its own, as I mentioned. To be brief,
back in the heyday of psychedelia, a New York
commune/rock band called the Group Image
rented the place and produced their own shows,
and owing to the success of those Group Image
shows, the ballroom became an off-and-on venue
for similar ventures. It had lain fallow for three
or four years, however, when Kiss arrived.

After a year of playing around the city, Kiss
had developed something of a following—if only
because they were a tough, sphincter-thumping
rock 'n' roll band when the other groups around
New York were ever more effeminate, ever more
arty. Furthermore, with their customary flair for
promotion—which may not have been sophisticated, but was undeniably ubiquitous—it's not too
surprising to learn that the Crystal Room at the
Dip was packed for their self-produced shows. It
was hot and uncomfortable in the room (though
compared to the scene at CBGB's today, it was
Shangri-la!). However, the balcony running three
quarters of the way around the room, the mirrored
walls, the faded elegance in general was just the

right ambience for developing a show that would owe a significant amount to horror movies. And the crowd loved it and began spreading the word.

The first Diplomat show took place on July 4, 1973, a day whose symbolism you can take as you will. Much more than their limited-attendance show at the loft in May, July Fourth represented the day Kiss was *really* born in the public's eye. And, just as every July Fourth celebrates our nation's independence, Kiss's July Fourth birthday celebrated *their* independence. The show was completely done by them on their own terms. As usual, the show was an umitigated success for the audience, but the music-biz invitees were not taking, this time around, and little did they know that they were blowing a very big shot.

August 10 was a hot and grimy day in New York City. People were escaping to the country, away from the pollution and the heat. Everywhere stores and restaurants on vacation displayed their "Gone Fishin' " signs. Nothing much in the city was open. And Kiss slugged along. They had business to do. Though they certainly couldn't have enjoyed the weather, they were looking forward to the evening with some relish. The night of August 10, 1973, they would present their second Diplomat show, and the band knew that those who were still left in New York would be looking for a ripping time.

Once again, the band had sent out scads of invitations to music people. Once again, they had sent one to the producer of *Flip Side*, Bill Aucoin. Once again, they didn't expect much response.

Still, they *believed*. Someday, their ship would come in.

Packing enthusiasm for the gig and a lifetime of hopes and dreams, Kiss straggled over to the Hotel Diplomat in the sleazy fringe area of Times Square. It was August 10, 1973, another dog day's night—and just another day that will live in infamy.

Chapter 3
Sparks Fly on Times Square

I've known I'm a star for a *long* time . . .
Gene Simmons, February 1976

To understand Kiss—their records, their concerts, their career—you have to hear about their manager. On August 10, 1973, at the Crystal Room of the Hotel Diplomat in steamy, summertime New York City, Bill Aucoin became the manager of the rock group Kiss, now known and loved around the planet. The concert that night was even more well attended than usual, which means it was a veritable "black hole of Calcutta" in the ballroom, and the band played a long, rousing set. As Bill Aucoin tells it, he was mightily impressed—though he had to be seeing a good deal beyond the ballroom. Despite the discomfort of the surroundings and the rough edges of the show—the makeup was nearly finalized but the show was almost a rag-tag, catch-as-catch-can parody of the multi-grand attraction it is today— Bill Aucoin was seeing the band's future, his future, and, most importantly (other pundits aside), the future of rock 'n' roll. He bobbed up and down to their raucous chords, and at the end of the set he offered to become their manager on the spot, and

44

if he couldn't secure a record contract within two weeks, all bets would be off.

The band was wary. They had been burned before. They were well aware of the pitfalls of the recording industry. So many sign management or recording contracts swathed in promises and wind up getting one thing after years for their troubles . . . those same promises. But the guy was so enthusiastic, so energetic, and he really seemed to mean it, *believe* it, when he told them he could help turn them into a "major act." The clincher for Kiss had to be that two weeks wasn't much of a chance to take after going at this full-tilt for a year—so they signed. And Aucoin was off and running with everybody's hopes, his own included, riding on the deal.

The bios note that Aucoin directed the nationally syndicated rock show *Flip Side* at the time. But I think it's highly unlikely that Aucoin was really taking home any serious cash from this small TV operation. Secondly, what the bios don't note is that Bill Aucoin worked as a unit director for another show before *Flip Side*, a show that some have compared his rock group to: namely, *Supermarket Sweep*, which was a ghastly low-rent *Price is Right*-cum-*Let's Make a Deal*, filmed on location at various supermarkets around the country. Now a unit director's job, no matter the show, is not an easy position and is generally well-salaried . . .

But it ain't a percentage of one of the biggest rock groups in the world!

No, I think it's safe to say that Bill Aucoin, who may one day be ranked as one of the all-time

great geniuses of show business, was scrapping
(comparatively) at the time, and saw much bigger, more important, and more lucrative things for
his life; I think it's safe to say that when Bill Aucoin encountered Kiss that August 10th at the Dip,
he had what is known in the "biz" as "desire"
(which, roughly translated, means the raw, lusting
energy to move mountains for a hit—or, at the very
least, get those mountains a recording contract).

   Which brings in Aucoin's friend Neil Bogart, a
story in and of himself. Best known in the sixties,
when he ran Buddah Records, as the King of Bubblegum Music, Bogart has been responsible for lots
that is and was, at the least, er . . . *interesting* in
the pop music field. Can *you* find a common
thread amongst the following: Question Mark &
the Mysterians, Terry Knight and the Pack, the
1910 Fruitgum Company, Curtis Mayfield, Mel-
anie, and the Isley Brothers? Give up? Well, for
one, a common thread amongst the first punk rock
group, the first bubblegum group, a singer-
songwriter, and a gospel group is that they were
all signed by Bogart, and after they became involved with Bogart they became very important
chart artists, i.e., Top 40 radio hit-makers. Add
Kiss to that list and you begin to realize that
Bogart either knows a trend when he sees one or is
able to make a trend when he feels like it.

   Anyway, Aucoin knew that Bogart was striking
out on his own from Buddah and was about to
form his own independent record label in Los Angeles that would be called Casablanca (from the
movie starring Humphrey *Bogart*, get it?). As yet
Bogart had signed no one, so Aucoin pitched Kiss

on the strength of his own opinion of the group, their talent, and perhaps above all their willingness to work hard, and Bogart went for it. Within the two weeks that Aucoin had promised, Kiss was signed—for the reported advance of ten thousand dollars. Kiss would be Casablanca's first—and, for quite a while, its only—signing.

Back in New York, the boys were well pleased. Ten thousand dollars was certainly not the biggest advance ever paid by a record company, but they knew that the advance is not the end-all of the game; in fact, as many groups will testify, the big advance can sink you before you begin. Once a record company has paid out six-hundred-thousand dollars to sign you, they may be hesitant to lay out any more for promotion, publicity, tour support, and the like. And those expenses are all-important—after all, no matter how good your album is, if nobody knows it exists, how are they going to find out they might like it? OK, so the advance paid to Kiss was a little on the low side. One has to realize that they were signed to a brand-new company with somewhat limited assets. One also has to realize that there are benefits to being the first signing to a record label. It can and did mean that at least for a while you—in this case Kiss—are the only concern of that company. In other words, what they didn't get in advance money was more than made up for in promotional attention. In fact, the cost of print space alone purchased by Casablanca for the group was huge.

So in August of '73 the group had a little cash and the promise of a lot of promotion. They also had a manager with the wherewithal to come through on the promises made so enthusiastically, as well as a theatrical and musical intelligence that jibed with their own. Over the next several weeks they would polish the music to everyone's satisfaction and then go in solidly rehearsed to a studio in New York to record the first Kiss album. Who could ask for more? Aucoin had done it!

But exactly *why* had Aucoin done it? Sure, as I've said, he was impressed by the gig at the Diplomat. But hadn't he been impressed by other groups? Weren't there—especially outside of the glitter/underground New York scene—more commercially viable groups to be had? Sure, he was impressed that they worked so hard, not only to please their audiences with a complete *theatrical* show, but to attract industry attention with their incessant and inventive mailing campaign. But weren't there a lot of musicians out there who were also hungry? Sure, Aucoin himself was at a point in his career where he was ready for the leap to super-success; sure, he was hungry, too. But why the sudden, the absolutely precipitous leap onto the Kiss bandwagon (actually more of a band-*cart* at that point)? For the answers I go back to the first time I met Aucoin, during Kiss's first tour.

Before a concert I was reviewing at San Francisco's Winterland, Aucoin invited me to a dinner. I found him to be a genial, intelligent man in his mid-thirties, a casual, if conservative, dresser in the preppie mode, sporting a mustache. For small talk we discussed our home town, New York, which, in spite of the beauty of San Francisco, we both missed.

Then I asked about Kiss.

Suddenly, he leans forward and his eyes blaze up. "Wait'll you see 'em," he says with surety. "They're amazing! They each have their own separate identities communicated through the makeup which they each developed themselves. They have a remarkable sense of theatrics. And this is where I see their place in rock." His brows knit. "You see, Alice Cooper has retired, at least for a while. He's going to be into movies and whole other areas. And he's going to be effectively out of the rock scene. He's very big, perhaps coming off the peak of his career right now. And with his retirement there's going to be a gap, a big gap. There is a need that Alice fulfilled, and with him out of the picture there's going to be this gap, which I think Kiss can step into and fill up again." I ask him if he's talking about the fact that with Alice's "retirement" (Alice's own word), there's going to be a dearth of theatrics in rock. "Yeah. People want to see a show. They've grown up. They've gotten spoiled by Alice. They want to see a complete show, which includes visuals. Kiss fulfills this desire, and I think they'll be very big."

Which is it—the reason Aucoin went head over heels for Kiss: He was an avid admirer of Alice Cooper and Alice's manager Shep Gordon, saw them as the future of rock, and when they bowed out he saw his opening—an opening that, given the average duration of show-biz retirements, might not be there for long. So he made his move and, with some luck, discovered Kiss. It's doubtful that today Aucoin would credit Alice Cooper's slide as the reason for Kiss's rise, but back in the spring of

'74, when I met manager Aucoin, the Alice Cooper connection was the fulcrum in his master plan. That night at the concert at Winterland the conservative Aucoin danced and bobbed like a teen-ager, frequently shouting in my ear, "Aren't they great?" There was no mistaking: He *believed*! in Kiss . . . *and* the Alice Cooper connection.

Things are moving fast in the early fall of '73, just like Aucoin wants them to. The band's repertoire has been edited to around a dozen songs polished to perfection, now to be worked on in the studio. This is not going to be any *Sgt. Pepper's* year-long epic adventure in recording tape and recording money. All anybody wants is an album of the best they can do at this moment in less than a month's time. Casablanca needs product. There will be time for *Sgt. Pepper's* later. First they must tour their asses off, let the people see them, build a grass-roots following. The album will basically serve as a reminder in the record store that this outrageous group Kiss does exist. If it sells, it sells. They won't start counting till the second or third one.

So in October of '73, Gene Simmons, Peter Criss, Paul Stanley, and Ace Frehley entered Bell Sound Studios, near West Fifty-seventh Street in Manhattan, to record the debut album, *Kiss*, with veteran efficiency-artists Kenny Kerner and Richie Wise producing, Warren Dewey engineering, and Bill Aucoin looking on proudly and protectively.

There was very little nervousness in the studio. There was some primping and dressing up among the band members, feeling out their newfound image as stars, but aside from that, little that would betray this as a debut effort. The fact of the matter was, of course, that Criss, Simmons, and Stanley had all recorded before, as I mentioned. So to a certain extent everyone here was a vet—excepting Ace, who compensated by being his usual fairly compliant, undeniably laid-back self—and so quite professional. Within three weeks they had a master tape. What some might call a minor masterpiece.

While the songs off their debut album, *Kiss*, have yet to be covered by Frank Sinatra, the material has certainly held up very well within the context of the current repertoire of the group: seven out of the ten songs on the first album were rerecorded live for the breakthrough *Kiss Alive!* But no matter how one chooses to measure it, this sometimes derivative, occasionally rough, occasionally faltering and remarkably overlooked first LP scores fairly high marks.

As with all their recordings, the secret of *Kiss* lies not in any one individual's accomplishments but in the work of the group *ensemble*. The elements that comprise the group Kiss in the studio at this point are: Simmons and Stanley's songwriting, both as a team and separate; Simmons's and Stanley's voices, again both apart and working together *and* with the rest of the group; Ace Frehley's instrumental punctuation, with his incisive solos and massive chordal asides; and lastly—but equally, to be sure—Peter Criss's trademark jungle drumming. All of which is not to mention Gene's spinal-tap bass style and Paul's subtly applied rhythm-guitar colors.

The album starts off very strong with a quadruple drumstroke from Criss into a power chord from Frehley (a move that foreshadowed "Rock and Roll All Nite," the atomic capacity hit forthcoming on a future LP) and on into the Simmons-and-Stanley-penned metallic vision of the coquette, "Strutter." From the classic title on down to the Who-like double-slash guitar strokes that open every verse, the song is a challenge to its coy female character, whose idea of foreplay is lots of come-on and lots more go-back. "Strutter," shouts lead vocalist Stanley in the chorus in a modulated anger that tells her he's hip to the game, while underneath him the bass throbs contradictory to his restraint.

"Strutter" is a masterpiece of the heavy-metal genre and, beyond that, stands aside from the pack and is one of those songs that make rock 'n' roll the all-important and pervasive social force it is today. "Strutter" reeks of frustration and anger and lashes out at both, becoming simultaneously a communication and thereby a release from black and destructive feelings. That it is a first cut of a first album by a new group is absolutely incredible. The fact that, many nights on the road, Kiss still open their show with this very song is testimony to their belief in its perennial effectiveness.

The *pace* of *Kiss* continues unabated into the next cut, if the intensity diminishes somewhat. Simmons's "Nothin' to Lose," another song still featured prominently by the group onstage, is again a missive to a woman, but whereas Stanley in "Strutter" was angry and put upon, Simmons in this song is cajoling—lasciviously, for sure (there are several fairly blunt and seemingly kinky sexual overtures)—but cajoling nonetheless, as sweetly as Simmons is likely capable of. Compared to the stridency of "Strutter," "Nothin' " fairly bounces along and, when it comes down to the last part with the group singing off-key harmonies a cappella, resembles nothing so much as some racy country-blues filler the Stones might put on their next album.

They've damned and they've cajoled, and in "Firehouse," the next tune, they reach a middle ground (for them), which is abject worship of the woman; as cleffer and vocalist Stanley assures us, he'll need the fire department to put out the "fire" this one has started in him. As many songwriters and groups do on their early outings, Stanley and Kiss cop their own riff on this cut. "Firehouse" is essentially "Strutter" with different lyrics—and one or two very telling musical details.

First of all, there's Ace's startlingly tense staccato solo in which he hangs on, striking one note repeatedly until the listener might think everybody will explode, only then releasing the note to travel on down the scale. Not since Neil Young's one-note, eight-bar solo on "Down by the River" had anyone pulled a song as taut as Ace does here, in his finest moment on the record (in fact one of the two finest moments in his career, the other being six albums later). The telling part of Ace's interlude is that less should never be expected from him—he could do it *all* from the start. The other musical detail goes back to my discussion of the importance of the Beatles in the grand scheme of things and in Kiss's expectations in particular.

Listen to the falsetto "woo-ooo"s that punctuate
the choruses. Do you remember the famous,
shriek-inspiring "woo"s from the Beatles' "She
Loves You"? If you do, you'll hear the connection: Kiss, who always wanted to be as big as
the Beatles, are musically touching base.

The three opening songs from the LP are the
important ones, the potential classics and the ones
that most convey the group's emerging identity.
Side one of the album finishes out with Ace
Frehley's only writing contribution, "Cold Gin,"
and Stanley's "Let Me Know." "Gin" is remarkable for Paul's terrific drunken vocal, which also
happens to sound a lot like the sloppy vocal from
another "cold" song about drug abuse, namely
(please note the Beatles connection again) "Cold
Turkey," by John Lennon. "Gin," unfortunately,
is not remarkable for Ace's solo work, "Let Me
Know" is unusual because it's one of the hap-
piest-sounding songs the group ever performed. At
one point the lyrics refer to a "bundle of joy," and
the a cappella singing at the end (you notice that
that was a favorite device) mimics a barbershop
quartet; while the delayed coda is a wild Yard-
birds-style changing-tempo rave-up, the overall effect of the song is almost straight music hall.

Side two of Kiss opens with what many con-
sider the band's worst song. Interestingly enough,
it was also their first single and a song that they
really laid their bets on. Who came up with the
idea to do "Kissin' Time" is unknown, but it's
likely that either management or the record company had the initial concept. That concept, a
faulty one as was well proven later, seems to have

been that they couldn't rely on the band's own songwriting for a hit single, so they copped Bobby Rydell's early '60s hit written by Mann and Lowe. When I received a copy of the single "Kissin' Time" before I had received the album, I was definitely put off from very high expectations. On the other hand, Gene Simmons seems to have gone along with the decision on the single. Said he in an interview at the time: " 'Kissin' Time' may just be our 'I Want To Hold Your Hand!' " (Again, note historical Liverpool reference . . . !)

The fact that Gene Simmons's "Deuce" follows "Kissin' Time," which is nothing if not an earlier, ersatz "Surfin' USA," on side two probably has nothing to do with the fact that the Beach Boys followed up *their* first hit with a song called "Little Deuce Coupe." At least, I don't think . . .

Actually, "Deuce" has nothing to do in any way with the Beach Boys' tune. The "deuce" of the Kiss song is either a two-dollar bill Gene's lover ought to surrender to him for "working" so hard, or the second time in a row she should avail him of her charms, likewise, for "working" so hard. "Deuce," which is thankful heavy-metal relief, in a Deep Purple mode, from the utter banality of its predecessor on the side, has become one of the thumpingly militant standards in the Kiss set. More than even "Strutter," which is not as proud, the lyrics to "Deuce" stand as a foreshadowing to the sexual braggadocio that has characterized the bulk of the group's songs through the years. If there were a need for such a movement, Kiss might be said to be "into" Men's Lib; and if the movement needed an anthem, "Deuce" might serve quite well.

Following "Deuce" are three songs that definitively mark the time at which this album was recorded: when the Allman Brothers and their trademark harmony-guitar playing was very big. "Love Theme from Kiss" (the only tune whose writing was ever credited to the entire band) is the first and last instrumental Kiss ever performed and a noble throwaway that features one brief guitar riff played in two-part harmony. "100,000 Years," a Simmons/Stanley composition, has lyrics —notably the word "bitch" periodically, in a refrain with nearly the braggadocio of "Deuce"—but churns on sluggishly and is highlighted by a harmony guitar solo only a bit better than the repeated figure of "Love Theme."

Stanley's "Black Diamond," which also showcases some dual guitar, is the most interesting of the three. For one, it opens as a ballad with Paul singing over two acoustic guitars, and leads from there into a metal stomp-'em-up (prefiguring Kiss's much later ballad success and their continuing intrigue with strong dynamic contrast). For another, "Black Diamond" waxes remarkably sensitive in its content, regarding both a *woman* (she's a streetwalker) and a *black* woman with a great deal of sympathy. The harsh doo-wop chorus betrays what may have influenced Stanley as he was writing "Diamond," namely, the Stones's then-current hit "Heartbreaker," which also featured an ironic doo-wop chorus and concerned the plight of urban blacks. In the end, however, the song can stand alone as a powerful and unique statement from the band, and remains a stalwart of their concert sets.

All in all, while the instrumental backing sometimes seems too thin, and the mix is fairly primitive even by the standards of 1973, and while the vocals could have used some polish in spots and the songs could have been more judiciously selected, Kiss's vinyl debut was and is very strong. In fact, the dearth of production values and overdubbing on *Kiss* comes through as an added strength in 1977, where the movement in recording, spearheaded by punk-rockers like the Ramones, seems to be towards a more basic, unadorned sound, more faithful to a band's actual live playing sound than to the sound a producer can coax from an electronic console. The group, Aucoin, and the record company were more than pleased.

So they had their record, but that was only the start. For such a strikingly visual group as Kiss, the clincher for success was going to be the touring. While the audience might ignore the likes of "Love Theme from Kiss" and, yes, perhaps even retch at "Kissin' Time," there was no way they'd ever forget those faces. With the album in the can, it was time to get those faces in front of the public. But where to start?

Now here's the area where Bill Aucoin may one day be recognized as a genius. From his training behind the scenes in television, he knew that what was needed at this point was what they've come to call a "media event." His and Bogart's dilemma was this: Which of the elements before him had "media attraction" and how could he "package" them for maximum exposure?

Well, for starters, Neil Bogart was launching a new record company; however, it wasn't a very big record company—in fact, it existed basically just on paper, not very big at all. So who's going to care? Aha! People will care when the smallest record company gives the biggest party. Secondly, Casablanca and Aucoin, under the aegis of his newly formed Rock Steady management company, were launching a new group. So who cares about unknown new groups? Aha! People will care when they're the most bizarrely costumed new group since—dare I say it?—Alice Cooper; and, in fact, never remove their whiteface makeup and never reveal their true identities. And people will care even more when the new record company, the new group, the outlandish makeup, the mysterious identities, and the lavish party are all rolled up into one big, glitzy package. One big show-biz "media event"!

The album was due for release in late February. The party happened in January. Herein I quote the lead lines from one of the lead items in a Los Angeles music magazine: "It's been the week for parties in Hollywood. Monday night Neil Bogart threw not so much a party, more of a major production for his newly formed Casablanca Records and their first signing, Kiss. . . . The affair was held in the grand ballroom of the Century Plaza Hotel—turned into a replica of 'Rick's Café' for the evening (from the film *Casablanca*)." So they all reported. The scam worked, as they say. The fact that Alice Cooper Himself showed up was only the ironic icing to everybody's cake.

In New York, the hometown of Aucoin and

the band, but merely an outpost to Casablanca
Records, the introduction of the press and Kiss
was only slightly less extravagant. Casablanca
rented the recently shuttered Fillmore East for the
band to perform and everybody to get happy on
lots of food and drink. Puns aside, the indulgent
rock press, in particular, ate it up. Again, the media
event worked—like a charm. But unbeknownst to
everybody involved, especially Casablanca, Rock
Steady, and Kiss, it would be the last thing to work
like a charm for some time to come.

Chapter 4
Bronx, 1999

> If it wasn't for the fact that I got into music, I'd have been hanging around the street corners getting in trouble . . . which is to say, my life was saved by rock 'n' roll.
>
> Ace Frehley, August 1975

To go any further without acknowledging that there are real, live faces underneath that Stein's Clown White greasepaint would be to lose something. It wasn't some bunch of leather-jacketed clowns that put together a promotional mailing list and produced their own gigs and finally recorded a near-brilliant rock 'n' roll album. It wasn't a group of freaky automatons who attended those glittering bashes in New York and Los Angeles and so geared up the press corps. And it wasn't—and *isn't*—four dressed-up empty shells that hit the road all over the world for nine months out of every year. No, it was—and it is—four people, four young men who have been doing all of this . . . and more. It is four young men who also have lives outside of a conglomerate called Kiss. It is four men who frequently get lost to everybody—fans, record company, management, even themselves—in the fast shuffle of their lives.

The point is, if what you are reading is to be nearly complete, these men have to be regained somewhat, for your sake and, perhaps ultimately, for the sake of the band members themselves. Can you begin to imagine what happens when you spend half your life for years on end wearing a face that you have invented? Can you imagine how it is to be recognized as your fantasy face and not as you, your real face, your real *self*? And what about the relationship you develop with your fantasy face? What about the relationship those close to you must have to develop with that fantasy face? Certainly all of this is greater than the trauma and confusion suffered by actors who are simply required to play a role, because they are not totally obscured by that role, nor can they possibly play it as frequently and as intensively as the members of Kiss do when they hit the stages of arenas around the world every other night in front of thousands of fans. Certainly there is no precedent for what Kiss must feel. And it is what they feel partially because we drive them to it, to giving us a show, to giving us an image. And these feelings, too, of course, come from within them, within what is behind those masks. That's what we're looking for.

Without his makeup, Ace Frehley is a bored, tough-looking kid. Not that at around twenty-six (he was born Paul Frehley, April 27 of a deliberately unknown year) Ace is a kid anymore, just that he does now and always will look like one. He's lanky. His skin is lightly pockmarked, and, since it rarely gets sun, is about the color of a fish underbelly—that is to say, of a bluish pallor. His eyes peer out from behind swollen cheekbones that deepen their brown color. His face is quite nearly the shape of this skull—narrow, coming to a square point at the chin. By his own description, Ace was a "tough kid" even when he was a kid. The swollen cheekbones and the hidden—and hiding—eyes were no accident of birth, exactly: They've been that way since the plasic surgeon operated to repair the disfigurement caused by a bottle smashed into the side of his face during a bar fight.

In his stocking feet—or in sneakers, his favored footwear, as I've seen him on occasion—Ace appears to be just shy of six feet tall, which would rank him third in descending order of true height of the band members, several inches above Peter. But his lack of stature is deceptive—Ace is the skinniest member of Kiss and seemingly the wiriest. All of which contribute to his punkish, tough-kid stance (check out his pose on the cover of *Dressed to Kill* for the archetypal Ace).

Like his eyes, Ace's manner is guarded. And not out of any fear, one feels, more out of the wisdom of experience—particularly with hurled bottles. He doesn't really say much voluntarily and doesn't seem too concerned with what's going on around him, though you know a man who plays like he does *is* concerned. Oh, he'll talk—especially after the couple of belts of hard stuff he is known to favor periodically. And what he has to say goes a lot of the way towards confirming what those Body Language people say about a person's bodily appearance betraying his inner self.

Ace's story is a punk's story—a tough past and a cavalier present—and his style, his choice of words, is a punk's style—noncommittal, disinterested, at least on the surface. Asked what he'll be doing in fifty years, Ace responds in a voice veiled with a raspy breath: "I don't know. What are you gonna be doin?" Will he be married? the interviewer inquires. "Probably," comes the one word non-answer. (Ace married, after this interview, his sweetheart, Jeanette.) Will he have kids? Again, he noncommits: "Probably." But when asked if he'll abandon guitars for his kids, he seems to get a little testy; obviously, the questioner is hitting home with that one. "No, I'll still have guitars. I'll *always* have guitars." And then, in an uncharacteristic move, he volunteers, "I'm also a painter. In my latter years, I'll probably go back to oil painting. I bet nobody knows I'm a painter. Right now my life is just too fast to really get into it." Is he good? the interviewer presses. "I'm adequate," says Ace, retreating a bit, but just a bit. "I designed the Kiss logo. I have artistic ability."

How does this tough guy view his current success? Cavalierly, how else? "I used to be a taxi driver and a mailman for eight months—if I was still a mailman I wouldn't be riding in a limousine." But aren't there any other benefits? "I'm fulfilled as a musician," he opines philosophically. "I always wanted to be a rock 'n' roll star when I grew up—at least, since I was thirteen. The Stones did it to me. I didn't really like the Beatles till I was eighteen. The Stones were rebels, and so was I! I started playing the guitar at fourteen, and actually the first song I played was . . . 'Mrs. Brown, You've Got a Lovely Daughter.' I got kicked out of two high schools, dropped out of a third, and finally went to night school. My first band was Four Roses . . . like the booze."

What about his friends? Were they the same?
Where are they now? "Half of my old friends,"
says the tough punk, playing the tough punk to
the hilt, "are dead now, or in jail. I used to hang
with a really rough crowd. One hung himself, a
couple OD'd, one or two are in jail." So how come
Ace made it? "Well, I'd probably still be there
with them, wherever they are, if it wasn't for the
fact that I got involved in music. Instead of hanging
out on street corners, getting in trouble, I started
practicing with a rock group. Which is to say," he
says with full drama, "my life was saved by rock
'n' roll."

To what does he attribute the success of the
band as a whole? "We have things to offer that no
other rock group does—I don't think I have to
mention any names; we all know who everybody
is. We're so uninhibited on stage, we make people
feel that way, too. I think they're uninhibited by
the paint, by the concert." How does the band
manage to get along so well, considering the travails
of road life and the like? Ace is asked. "I think
'cause we're realistic enough to realize that we've
done something that not many groups can do in
such a short time," he states evenly, one of the more
sober responses of the interview. "We're all mature
enough to realize that we must get along—because
we don't want to blow it. I think if things were
going wrong we'd be getting along a lot worse."

It's clear that Ace isn't posing when he says he
enjoys his success and that it has changed his life,
both in terms of money and in terms of some very
important relationships. "I buy luxuries I couldn't
afford before. Jewelry and nicer clothes. And I

now have five guitars." And later he adds: "I get along better with my parents now, because I used to be a bum with no steady job. And I was always getting in trouble in school because I didn't care, because I always felt I was going to be a rock 'n' roll star. I sensed I would be famous, always had the feeling. But nobody would believe me—even up until two years ago. A few months before Kiss began, I got into an argument with a girl friend. She was saying, 'Get a job! Get a job!' And I was saying, 'I can't! Don't you understand? I'm going to be famous one day! I'm going to be rich!' She looked at me like I was out of my mind. To this day, she remembers that and she says, 'You know, you were right, you were really sensitive.' "

Of course, the little incident with his girl friend probably cheered Ace a lot—you get the feeling that the punk thinks he's always right. I mean, when he lists his favorite movie stars, the list starts off with "Bogie, Paul Newman, and George C. Scott," which is not the kind of bunch who think they're ever wrong, nor do they like to be told they are.

Like I said at the outset, there are people under all that makeup. But what kind of relationship do they have *with* their painted-on faces? What does "Space" Ace feel about the public performer Ace? And will he and the band ever take the makeup off? Well, for one, the identity of Ace, shrouded in mystery as it is, fits his personality quite well, though, I think, there is a distortion, in the on-stage persona, of where that personality comes from. Ace *is* "spaced out," somewhat uncommunicative, noncommittal, seemingly noncaring, as I've described, but it's *not* because he truly comes from another planet—it's because he comes from another planet in his mind. Getting back to the "borough mentality" discussion, Ace comes from the tough street corners of the Bronx, comes from another planet, *compared to where he is now.* However, where the fantasy persona of Ace onstage is of a person who descended to Earth, the reality personality of the man is that he ascended from Earth to the stars, from the Bronx to Kiss. Either way, it's a huge distance. As to taking the makeup off, Ace says this: "If it's advantageous to us, we'll do it. I don't know if it's a good idea, so I'll leave it to our manager [Aucoin] to decide. I think we have a mystique about us, and I think it might be a mistake." What about people on the street? Are they fooled when Kiss is not wearing makeup, or can they recognize them? "People know who we are," Ace replies cockily. "They can sense it. You can sense a star whether he has makeup on or not. We all have a charisma about us, almost a magic, that people can pick up on. They know you're not just a person—but somebody special."

Special, yes. But very elusive. Not only do they not appear before an audience or allow photos without full makeup, they don't permit the public to know the year they were born, and they never use their real names. To profile the band as a unit is one thing, but to put together individual bios of the members is another. You have to take all the clues you can find to solve the mystery of Kiss.

One overlooked clue is their handwriting, in particular the revealing signatures which are affixed to their "Notes" on the inside of the jacket of *Alive!* and on their concert program. We analyze politicians by their handwriting and police uncover criminals' personalities by their handwriting, so why not rock stars? Since we've been talking about Ace, let's look at his signature (reproduced here) and see how it jibes with everything else that he appears to be in "real" life:

As is the case with most performers, Ace's signature is a big one, it takes up a lot of space. Part of the reason for this among performers is that they are accommodating fans who want a larger-than-life signature from their heroes, and part of the reason is that the performers actually do see themselves as larger than life. Look closely. Ace's signature is essentially laid out in a vertical space—that is, the letters go up and down more than they go from side to side. On the inner jacket to *Alive!*, for example, compare Ace's sign-off to that of the rest of the band; here the difference is the most clear-cut; specifically, *Ace doesn't even sign his last name!* In the concert program, while his name still occupies the least space horizontally of any of his associates, he does sign his last name. But look at that signature—you can hardly read anything beyond the *Fre* (trying to emphasize "free" perhaps?) of his last name. It looks as if he is working against some invisible boundary, lengthwise, and so accommodating by jamming the *h*, the *l*, and the second *e* together.

What does this all say about Ace Frehley, the person? Well, I think it holds true to the image of the street tough. For one thing, Ace is no less demonstrative about his signature—he does write it large—however, he does not like to stretch it out—just like he doesn't seem to like to stretch out in a personal encounter. He is reticent, he holds back, he reels his lines into a tight space. And it is such a tight space, both in which he contains his signature and, too, I think, his emotions, that it all threatens to explode. When the emotions therefore are let out, they are likely let out by an explosion—an explosion that might very well take the form of a searing, slashing guitar solo that literally *itself* explodes when Ace unleashes those skyrockets from the neck of his guitar. And isn't it the stereotypical way for the street tough of fact and fiction to deal with his feelings? To play them close to the vest, to be cool . . . until he *just goes berserk.*

Another thing about Ace's signature is that it is simultaneously the most illegible of the band members' signatures and also the most genuinely artistic. Being illegible is both something that would follow from a punk's way of thinking and something that might follow from the mind of an artist. Perhaps this is a dichotomy in Ace's personality, but I prefer to think it bespeaks a rich duality. He is the punk who doesn't care if anybody can read his signature. "I'm me, man," is what he might be saying, "and you don't need no more proof than that." He is also the artist who attempts to give his viewers a different, a unique way of seeing things. It's not just the letters, the words that matter, the artist believes, it's also how the words are presented visually. This latter would seem to fit in with his onstage persona as "Space Ace"—he sees things not as we do here on earth, but in a different way—through the prism of millions of miles of space (a space, we have established, which need not be "outer" space). It also fits into his statement that some time in the future he might like to return to the oil painting he has been neglecting since his cosmic induction into Kiss.

From all that can be gleaned from interviews and various investigative analyses of Ace Frehley, it's clear that while he may not actually be from somewhere other than this earth, he is a deceptively complex person and almost as hard to fathom as any Martian. You might think, from the veiled eyes, the nearly masklike features of Ace offstage, from the gritty breathiness of his voice and the New York accent, from the offhand manner in which he casts his lanky body about, that here's another New York street tough, maybe a kid who likes to get drunk and steal cars and eventually winds up doing fifteen months at the juvenile center. And you might almost be right. Because from what he's said about his Bronx background, from what can be observed about him now—the residual Bronx-ness of his being—that seems to have been one of his options in life. Fortunately, for us and for Ace Frehley, it's an "almost" statement, hypothetical. The reason—to paraphrase his own words—is that: *His life was saved by the greatest rock 'n' roll group in history, Kiss.*

Perhaps, too, that statement can be run vice-versa. I mean, couldn't it be that *Kiss, the greatest rock 'n' roll band in history* was also to a certain extent *saved by Ace Frehley's life?* I think so. I think that like the Beatles, who at one time they emulated and who now they ironically threaten to bury, the story of Kiss would not be the same without all the members, the very individual parts who make up that story. Without a guy named Ace Frehley from the Bronx, a guy they lovingly refer to as "Mr. Excitement" because he is so laid-back most of the time, Kiss might have wound up the much more typical rock 'n' roll story: up (with a hit single), down (without a follow-up hit), and out. I think that without the steady and tough cool of Ace, street punk and artist, not to mention Ace's ability to explode onstage with guitar licks as white-hot as the reentry shield of any spacecraft, and without the spaceyness that led him to become the extraterrestrial persona of the band, Kiss might have been a good band—but not a great one.

On record, on the road, onstage and off, that seems to be the story: Kiss is Kiss, and not Simmons, Stanley, Frehley, and Criss.

Chapter 5
Cat As Cat Can

It's funny. I don't feel like a star, and I think maybe that's good—because if I did, I might go crazy.

Peter Criss, July 1975

If Ace is elusive by force of habit, Peter Criss is elusive by instinct. Of course, he is that mercurial creature, the Cat. He's the Cat—but is he the lovable, cuddly, domesticated kitty-cat? Or the predatory jungle warrior? Is he the alley cat that shrieks all night on the back fence in the rancid urban bypasses? Or is he that cat of the ancient Pharaohs of Egypt, that mysterious silky being that they believed held powers divine and otherwise?

If the truth be known, he is all these things and more. And, any way you type him, the Cat has been around for five thousand years.

Which is odd. Because actually Peter (real name: Peter Crisscoula), born on December 20, is the oldest member of Kiss, being comfortably into his early thirties. He is also the only member of Kiss with gray hair—since Ace stopped painting his. The fact of the matter is that Peter shows his greater age in many more ways than his hair. Peter, I believe, is the most even-tempered and mature of all the members of the band, and well he

72

should be, it's been a maturity hard won. But, true to cat form, he has at last landed on his feet. But before that, it was . . . well, truly cat as cat can.

Peter comes from Brooklyn, near where Gene's family, curiously enough, originally lived. His family was hardly wealthy, and so young Peter—the kitten—attended Catholic schools in the area. When queried on the subject of his parochial-school experiences, he demurs, like so many Catholics who find the memory of rigid discipline and harsh religiosity of parochial schools a little too heavy to handle in small talk. Peter admits: "Someday I want to write a book about it." Peter is the only one in the band to acknowledge having gone to Catholic schools. He's the only one to have really grown up in the fifties—that era everyone seems to remember so fondly these days, even those who couldn't be old enough to have a real inkling of what it was like. In a lot of ways, then, Peter's background is almost unique among the stars who emerged in the seventies. Let me explain.

Catholic schooling and the fifties—to me they almost go together as one unified concept. Before the Ecumenical Councils held in the Vatican in the mid-sixties, the Catholic Church was conducting services and educating children much the same way they had done for over a thousand years. In the services, the priest faced the altar (as opposed to today, when he faces the congregation) and spoke entirely in Latin—except for a brief few phrases he spoke in Greek. To truly understand the service you had to know your Latin—and a smidgen of Greek, to boot. Which few people—and certainly not schoolchildren—did. In other

words, going to Mass back in pre-Ecumenical
times was a mysterious and even frightening experience. And it was required that the parochial
school kids—like Peter—attend every day. But
that's just the half of it.

In the classroom, the nuns required that children follow all the rules that any school kid of the
time followed, to a greater or lesser degree, I sup-
pose, depending on the school. But where the ultimate punishment for the public school kid who
transgressed was perhaps some form of the dunce
cap or, at worst, a paddling, the kid in the Catholic
school had to not only accept earthly punishment
but was frequently reminded of the Divine punishment that might be likely to follow . . . someday
. . . In other words, as they say in those hot dog ads
on TV, the Catholic school kid had to answer to a
higher authority. Sure, there were public schools
that were strict, and parents that were even strict-
er—but nobody wielded the authority that God
did in parochial schools in the 1950s! And that's
Who Peter Criss was up against. Which is probably why he has said: "I like the drums because
they release my frustration." Catholic school in the
fifties was a pretty frustrating situation for a kid
to grow up under.

And when I say under, I mean it: Even today,
Peter is the shortest member of his group, standing
in his sneakers at around five feet eight inches.
Which, when you're a poor kid growing up in
Brooklyn in the fifties, has got to be part of the rea-
son you're determined to prove yourself.

Drums wasn't the only way Peter let out his frustrations. There were the gangs—about which Peter

allegedly made one fairly outrageous claim: "We used to beat up Gene and his friends." He went on to explain. "It was really bad where Gene and I grew up. I had no other choice but to be in a gang—but I liked it because it was the closest thing to being an outlaw. You had a chance to dress up and hang out and all the chicks dug you 'cause you were like Marlon Brando. I was in real rumbles, too, and I've got the scars to show it. It was exciting, but it was scary. I still didn't like it that much because I still wanted to be a star. I still wanted to be in a rock 'n' roll band." Not that being in a rock 'n' roll band was a tame thing to do—not in the Fabulous Fifties. Contrary to popular image, everybody in the fifties and the early sixties was not running around in a black leather jacket and a ducktail and putting together rock 'n' roll bands. No, the people in the leather and the people in the bands—not one and the same group, necessarily—were the outcasts, "outlaws," to use Peter's word, and by far the minority of teenagers. To join a band back then, no matter what music you were playing, meant you were becoming a musician. And a "musician" was conceived of as a person apart, a fringe character, perhaps very artistic, perhaps very eccentric, certainly weird and probably involved with drugs, notably Mariwanna, the killer weed. An appropriate analogy might be that most people—teen-agers included—in the fifties and early sixties viewed musicians (no matter how much they enjoyed their music) much the same as hippies viewed businessmen during the Summer of Love several years later: they were weirdos. Period.

So Peter got himself a set of 1920s drums (not unlike those played by Gene Krupa himself) from the money he made as a delivery boy, and settled down to practice, eventually landing in a band called the Barracudas. Now he was a musician. And while gangs and black leather jackets were sometimes a passing phase for even the most wonderful of teen-agers, people knew, a musician was a musician. Henceforth, Peter would be a "weirdo" or, if you prefer, an "outlaw." For the next ten years he would be playing clubs—"every club in New York City," he says—weddings, and bar mitzvahs. First, he was interested in Gene Krupa, an interest inspired by his father's swing music records. So after the Barracudas he hooked up with a society band, which might be a stultifying environment for a budding young drummer, who also likes to sing and compose, but which was certainly good for discipline. Fortunately, though, he graduated from the society band and played in a serious jazz combo. Then there was a Latin band and, for the longest time, a soul group with brass.

But sometime in there the image of the musician changed. It wasn't the Beatles that happened for Peter, it was the Rolling Stones. Did I say the image of the musician had changed? Well, not exactly, perhaps it would be more correct to say that the image and many of the musicians sort of came out of the closet, saying "We're outlaws, and we're going to put it right in your face! And your gonna like it, or go to hell!" Certainly that's what the Stones seemed to say. They were scruffy, their music was scruffy. They were out-front rebels— and precisely what Peter and millions of other teen-agers had been looking for. Peter wanted to be as big and bad as the Stones. To this end he wanted to start playing originals in his bands, get a real solid rock 'n' roll unit together. No more bar mitzvahs! The exodus is here!

Finally he hit on a band called Chelsea (not after New York's Chelsea neighborhood, but after London's Chelsea, rock bands being anglophiles in those days). Little is known about the group; no one we know has ever heard their music. But Chelsea was a rock 'n' roll unit playing originals, and eventually they landed a contract on Decca Records and made an album, a move which for those days was like reaching the moon. But the moon it wasn't—the record was lucky if it reached the bargain basement racks. Peter blames a "schmuck manager," a "schmuck producer," and the lack of financial backing, but the hard cold fact of the matter is that Chelsea broke up and with it a lot of Peter's hopes and dreams. It would be two years before anything else would come along.

And what about those two years? Peter has indicated that they were among the most painful of his life. Married to his lovely wife Lydia by this time, Peter, the only kid on the block with a record contract, essentially had to start from scratch. Imagine his humiliation—he, the drummer from Chelsea, having to answer ads in *Rolling Stone* and the *Village Voice*. Well, it sent Peter for the most part spinning into depression.

Despite the fact that he was practicing a lot during this period, he knew he was still back at the starvation level of existence. He wanted to do originals—he knew he was a star—but in the meantime he also had to make some bucks. Towards his *big* goal he placed an ad in *Rolling Stone*, and, on the other hand, towards making some bucks *quick* he hooked up with a couple of groups and started doing clubs again. "I got really depressed," he told one interviewer. "I started getting high, and it got to the point where the only way I could do it was stoned." This depressing situation continued on and off through the two years, forging all the time a Peter Criss more determined to make it. He placed another ad in *Rolling Stone*—nothing. And then he gave it one more try with ad copy that was to the point. "Drummer willing to do anything to make it," read the classified. Then came the fateful response. . . .

"Gene called me while I was having a party," Peter has reported. "Everybody was smashed. I picked up the phone and he says, 'Hi.' I was the first drummer he had called. Then he says, 'Listen. First of all, are you thin?' I put the phone away from my ear and ask the party, 'Hey, guys, am I thin?' and everybody says, 'Yeah,' and I say to Gene, 'Yeah, I'm thin.' Then he goes, 'Do you have long hair?' And I say, 'Do I have long hair?' and everybody says, 'Yeah, yeah!' So I tell him yeah. Then he asks me if I'm good looking and I say to everybody, 'Am I good looking?' And you could hear all these people hysterical. So I say, 'Yeah, I'm really cute.' Then he wants to know how long I've been playing, and I tell him 'a really long time and I'm looking to make it—and I want to do originals.' " The agreement was then struck that Gene with Paul would meet him later that week in front of Electric Ladyland Studios

(built by the late Jimi Hendrix) on Greenwich
Village's notorious Times Square-style muck-
hole-south, Eighth Street. Peter tells the rest:

"That day I went to the Village with my
brother and really got *dressed*, wearing this jacket
I bought in England and a red satin shirt and a
black velvet pants—I really looked nice. And there
were these two guys—later I found out they were
Gene and Paul—who had asked *me* how *I* dressed,
standing outside the Lady with these flower shirts,
looking like they came from the days of Gracie
Slick and the Jefferson Airplane. I passed them up
because they didn't even look like anybody. I got
into Electric Ladyland and ask a guy if Gene and
Paul are there and he says, 'Yeah, they're right outside.' I look outside and say, 'That's *them*! And
they asked me if *I dressed*!'

"I said I was Peter Criss to them, and we all
went inside and found out that people they were
involved with were people I had been involved
with a couple of years before. So it was kind of a
freaky circle—we knew some people but never each
other. Anyway, I heard their tape and I liked
them. It wasn't exactly what I wanted to do, but
it wasn't exactly what they wanted to do either.
We had a rehearsal . . . The first rehearsal was a
disaster—we didn't hit it off right away—but the
second one was great! So the three of us rehearsed
for five to six months—we didn't want to get a guitarist till the rhythm section was tight. We rehearsed seven days a week, eight hours a day. Then
Ace came in—you should've seen some of the win-
ners we auditioned!—he came in one night and the
three of us knew immediately . . ."

Again, there it is in Peter's speech, that mystical reference to knowing immediately, that cat instinct for what is right, how and where to land so you wind up on your feet, the deep inner cat knowledge that impelled him ultimately to join up with Gene and Paul and form Kiss and then paint his face in the manner of a cat.

And how does his handwriting relate to the personality of Peter Criss?

Consulting the inner "Notes" from *Alive!* once more, it's readily apparent that Peter's handwriting is the least studied of all the members of the group. Even his signature—which he must have signed fifty thousand times in the past several years—seems almost slapdash. Granted it is fairly consistent at this point—and *nota bene*: he always employs the double-lightning-bolt S's—but it remains a series of broad separate strokes that rarely interlock and rarely become more than printing. While Ace Frehley crams his John Hancock into one horizontally restricted logotype image, Peter puts his letters down one by one—each one allowed to stand completely by itself—almost as if he doesn't care from one stroke to the next where each letter lands. The fact of the matter is: He doesn't care, he *knows*. He is, as we have established, the Cat. He can be thrown or jump from any cockeyed angle and always come up with all four—make that *two*: let's not get carried away—feet absolutely on the ground, as he has shown throughout his life. From

HEADS UP,
FLAMING YOUTH!
HITHER COMETH
THY DESTINY!

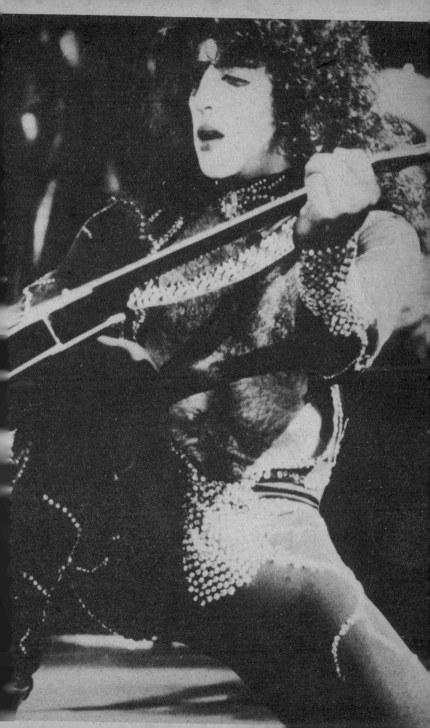

the back alleys of Brooklyn in the fifties to the front alleys of a posh post-concert party in New York, the Cat has prowled—or "stalked" as he refers in *Alive!*—and always come out in balance.

Peter Criss, the Jungle Cat pounding his jungle rhythms. Peter Criss, the rhinestone-studded god-cat of Ancient Egypt. Peter Criss, the simultaneously lovable and inscrutable little round feline represented on his "fan" note in the live LP. He is all these cats and he is The Kitty-Kat of Kiss. Who else could they hoist twenty feet in the air and expect to come down right?

Chapter 6
Stardust Confidential

> We put our asses on the line to do this.
> Paul Stanley, November 1976

And what an ass it is! Certainly—as Paul might readily, if somewhat shyly, admit—his ass is a large measure of what Paul Stanley has to add to the heady brew in the Kiss Kauldron.

But not all—in all seriousness—not by a long shot.

Roughly estimating, Paul Stanley has been responsible for writing half the songs in the Kiss repertoire, and is responsible for the lead vocal on more than that. As rhythm guitarist, he should be and is the rock-bottom foundation for a group that plays it very hard and fast. All of which is not to mention that Paul Stanley, with Gene, is one of the cofounders of the band. In a sense he is both the brains *and* the beauty behind Kiss, sort of like Kate Hepburn in *Woman of the Year*. And as with Hepburn in that movie, you better not be deceived by the wrapping—there's a lot to tangle with in that package.

I throw that analogy in because I'm aware that when it comes to Paul, all the fans can think about is S-E-X. And at this juncture in the heaven-bound career of this band, it may just be that Paul is ready to take his place alongside such great American symbols as Hepburn or, on the masculine side, Clint Eastwood. But what the hell, let's get down to sex.

The gender confusion of the above paragraph is nothing less than intentional—because the gender confusion of Paul Stanley is nothing less than intentional. His hairy chest and swarthy, well-muscled torso immediately nails him as a macho stud of the first order, definitely of the Mediterranean school of lovers (Marcello Mastroianni, for instance), while his smoothly contoured legs and face, especially the face, mark him as something again altogether. His thick ruby-red lips are constantly pursing beneath the high, proud cheekbones. Unlike the others in the band, Paul's makeup is less another identity than an embellishment of his own features—certainly Paul is the easiest one to recognize without makeup. His face is mostly white, only his eye is decorated in black with the star that, were it not painted there, might still be visible. His makeup does not so much hide as highlight, and what it highlights is the distinctly *pretty* attributes of Paul Stanley.

Part of the reason Paul Stanley seems an ambivalent character—at once tough masculine and precious feminine—is that Kiss was born at the time when neo–Alice Coopers were absolutely the dominant force on the New York music scene. Of course, gender confusion had preceded Alice in rock (for one thing, the rumor was frequently circulated in 1965 that Mick Jagger was about to undergo a sex change; people thought Jagger was outrageously feminine!), but not till Alice did it

all start to truly emerge from the closet. The movement in rock towards dressing female—or, at least,
dressing to confuse—even got a name, became its
own genre, called Glitter Rock. And Glitter is
when Kiss was born.

Again, as I've explained, the band started out on
that course with very feminine makeup and clothes
but soon drew away, sensing the dead-endness of
the move. It was a wise move because they *did*
look ridiculous in that female stuff—that is, all except for Paul. Without makeup it's readily apparent
that Paul *is* the best-looking one in the group; so
when the band went to leather and steel, Paul could
change his costume but keep his makeup. The fact
was, it actually looked *good* on him. And if they
were going to call themselves Kiss, *somebody*
ought to have big red lips to help identify the band
visually. So Paul became the visual touchstone for
the group name, and became the *touch*stone for
millions of righteously randy fans. But if all this
sounds real casual, just like Paul *fell* into his role as
sex symbol, it isn't.

First of all, Paul was born (January 20, circa
1950) in Queens. Stop. Period. Think back to the
discussion in chapter two of Queens. Think. Now
do you get it? That's right. Queens, as I said back
then, is just about as nowhere as you can get—at
least in terms of popular opinion around the New
York metropolitan area. One does not grow up in
Queens and automatically start thinking, acting, or
feeling like a sex symbol. More likely, one grows
up in Queens feeling like a schlub.

Like the rest of the band members, Paul does not
come from a musical or even a show-biz family.

His father runs a furniture store in Queens. Not
that dad doesn't have a lot of the show-biz instinct
in him. At the party after their triumphant
Madison Square Garden show in the spring of '77,
Mr. Eisen (Paul's real name is Stanley Eisen)
sidled over to us and became quite voluble about
Paul's success. "Paul is *very* talented," he mused
aloud. "You know, he can paint, too!" And Mr.
Eisen went on and on, quite charmingly, about
how multifaceted Paul is (yes, even he calls him
"Paul" now—at least in public). In fact, we did
wonder how you turned him off. Anyway, it became clear that his son comes by his need to show
off—albeit pleasantly and imaginatively—quite naturally.

Wanting to show off doesn't, however, make you
a star. In Paul's case, far from it. He was a fat
teen-ager and simply not that appealing. He told
one interviewer: "I looked like I was put together with spare parts! Like somebody said, 'Hey,
here's a set of legs—stick 'em on!'" He told me: "I
was a loser in high school, an outcast. I was a little
guy, stubby, overweight. I was the kid who
wasn't invited to the parties—and now I throw the
parties. It's always nice to know who gets the last
laugh." He knew he was fairly smart—he did all
right in high school, by his own admission, "always at the bottom of the smartest class." But nothing spectacular. *Except*: "I always knew I was
gonna be a star." Echoing the feelings of his associates in Kiss, Paul traces his intimations of his own
stardom back to very early in life. "I knew I was
gonna be a star probably from when I was five
years old. I used to watch American Bandstand

and Alan Freed. More than anything, I wanted to
be a rock 'n' roller. I always wanted to be a rock
star and I always knew I would be. It's just
knowing you're capable of it, a matter of realizing
you are capable of anything you want to do. Most
people don't give themselves much credit, they
don't have that high an opinion of themselves."
Did I mention *desire* in Queens? This fat boy had
it in spades!

It would be long years of hard work and frustration before that desire would be fulfilled, however.
As he told Frank Rose of *Circus* magazine, "I was
an art student and wanted to become a commercial
artist. But I just couldn't stand people expecting
things of me . . . Little by little I moved from art
and into music. I got into guitar because nobody
around me—especially my parents—took it seriously. I could go into my room and play guitar for
eight hours and nobody would bother me." But
besides the frustrations at home, there were the
frustrations of dealing with his peers, with whom
he had trouble communicating. You see, Paul knew
a lot about rock music, particularly focusing on the
English sound that was sweeping the country in
'64–'65. He knew and liked all the big name
bands—Stones, Who, Yardbirds, Kinks, and Small
Faces (later, The Faces With Rod Stewart). But
also, he told *Circus*, he was into "a lot of unknown
English bands. . . . Most of the kids in the neighborhood were into Top 40. We couldn't see eye to
eye."

To meet a need for material, one supposes, Paul
started writing his own songs when he was "fourteen or fifteen." But, naturally, that material

wouldn't wash with the high-school-prom crowd. In 1964 or '65 they wanted Beatles, Stones, Paul Revere and the Raiders, and surfing music. So essentially that's what he wound up playing—whatever was popular—working on his originals in his spare time. Believe it or not, this condition continued for almost five years. Then he met Gene.

As far as can be deduced, it was about 1970 and they both wound up playing in the same band and sensing similar ambitions in each other. Paul told an interviewer: "After a while we really solidified the concept of what we wanted to do. We didn't want to hard-rock one minute and country [Country??? Can you imagine???] the next to show everybody how versatile we were. We wanted to specialize. And at the very beginning we wanted to wear some kind of stage clothes. . . . The people we were playing with didn't want to have anything to do with that. . . . So we knew it was time to split."

Where they split to is difficult to trace, as is the case with all Kiss data, but within the next two years they had formed the band that would record that tape for Columbia that is still in the vaults somewhere. From what I understand of the Great Lost Simmons-Stanley Mystery Tape, it was definitely an affair written and orchestrated by Gene and Paul. It was recorded at Electric Lady—as I found out in a roundabout way during this snatch of conversation with Paul about Eddie Kramer: "Gene and I knew Eddie Kramer for years and years and years. He used to work at Electric Lady pretty exclusively. And when I was eighteen, Gene and I were going to work at Electric Lady with

another group, and Eddie was the house producer—
however, *not* for us; he was ten steps above us!" It's
likely that it was heavy metal. But that's pure specu-
lation. One hopes that someday that tape will surface for general consumption. Till then we can only
dream—that we find it *ourselves*.

But after that tape—and partially as a result of
the advance money they earned from that tape—
came the long search for the right mix that would
form Kiss—and, ultimately, success beyond Paul's
wildest fat gurgling dreams.

Paul puts heavy importance on the role his relationship with band and songwriting partner Gene
has played in their skyrocketing fame and for-
tunes. He told an interviewer about the balance
they have established: "Gene and I are very
strong. So it's important to realize what you can do
with each other and what you can't. Because with
two such strong personalities, I imagine they demand a lot of attention, and we both realize that
you can't divide something like that up. It works
that way with the whole band. That's what makes
us so successful—we realize what we can and can't
do with each other, and we're that considerate of
the other guy and ourselves."

How does Paul relate to himself and the band in
makeup and onstage? Confirming much of what has
been discussed here, he responded this way, to one
reporter: "Kiss onstage is our personalities mag-
nified much larger."

During the recording of *Rock and Roll Over* in
the fall of '76, I spent some time with Gene and
Paul in the studio, and I believe captured some revealing and pretty strong statements from them. To

further explore Paul's relationship to the band and
his music, and also to allow the reader to just hear
Paul talk, I'd like to excerpt some of that here now
(from my article in *Creem*), along with some of my
questions to him at the time and some parenthetical
explanations of our comments:

Is it true that you're trying to discredit *Destroyer*
(because it wasn't as popular with the letter-writ-
ing fans, "too slick," though it did go platinum)?
I asked Paul.

"People try to read into things," he responded.
"Kiss has never been anything but a right-on-the-
line, straightforward rock 'n' roll band. So many
people said, 'Look what's happened to them.
They've become successful and they're forsaking
rock 'n' roll.' But *Destroyer* sold a million copies.
I don't knock that album. I think productionwise
it's an excellent album. But it's not an album I
would like to do twice.

"Once we had finished that album we were very
excited to do another. It was like we had to get it
out of our systems, and we learned a lot. Bob Ezrin
[the producer, formerly produced Alice Cooper]
is a very interesting guy to work with. We were
going through a time then when we weren't sure
what we wanted to do, and we wanted to work
with someone who could act as a catalyst. By the
time we finished that album, we had very strong
feelings about what we wanted to do with the next
one, and it shows."

What do you want to do? I continued.

"An excellent classic rock 'n' roll album," Paul
said. "There's no strings on this album. There's no
choirs, no keyboards, all guitars.

"This album is a return to the essence of what Kiss has always gotten off doing. These songs kick ass, no two ways about it. They're lethal. They're heavy guitar songs. *Alive!*, that is Kiss. That's the total summation of Kiss. *Alive!* is what we stand for. This album I see as a follow-up to *Alive!*"

To which I agree wholeheartedly, more on which in a later chapter.

I want to know now if Kiss will endure. It's been thirteen years from the Beatles' and the Stones' beginning, and clearly they have stood the test of time. I ask Paul if people will still be listening to *Alive!* in ten years. He thinks a moment and then begins to speak very sincerely in his somewhat muddled, New York accent: "I know that some of the songs on that album still knock me out as much as ever. I know *I* love 'Strutter,' and that in ten years *I'll* still be listening to 'Strutter.'" And then he pauses to reflect again for a moment. He is very serious. "*Kiss Alive!* is an album you could give to somebody and say, 'This is rock 'n' roll.' The album *is* rock 'n' roll. It's like a synthesis of everything I wanted to hear in rock 'n' roll. That's why I like it—'cause I'm a big fan of our influences, English bands like the Move, Stones, Kinks, Yardbirds, Pretty Things, and Zep."

But what will Paul Stanley be doing otherwise in ten years? At this, he cracks up, revealing an easy and friendly sense of humor. "What, you wanna date?" he queries back. Can you play heavy-metal rock 'n' roll for ten years? I continue. "I can play for ten years," he opines, "but what it'll sound like in ten years, who knows? You can't stop evolving."

Getting back to this side of Paul, I tell him I think he has a sense of humor about what he does. He answers simply, unequivocally: "Absolutely." Then Kiss is not that serious? I press. "Nothing's that serious. If you can't laugh, then you have a real problem. The fact that I can joke about it doesn't mean I'm not that serious about it. The fact that it's fun doesn't make it any less valid. Hey, we put our asses on the line to do this. At the beginning, we did it because we believed in it. Not because it was a joke. And it's no more of a joke now."

There was lots more banter—Paul is very easy to talk to. He's always willing to play along. When I asked him about platform shoes, he joked about the Frye boots he was wearing that day; he told me he likes to write songs standing up and blasting his guitar. Then I asked if the band would take off the makeup for their next tour, attempting to sneak a scoop statement out of him. He's alert: "No way! We'll know when the time is right. We don't want to do it yet. We like what we're doing. That doesn't mean in five years we'll still be doing it. Do you want us to take it off? I don't look much different with or without makeup, just a little paler with the makeup on. Taking the makeup off would be like changing the instrumentation—it's a part of Kiss. We'll do it when we feel it's the right time or when our audience really wants it."

At the end of our formal talk, which lasted about an hour, we were all laughing and joking about Kiss and music and New York, but I thought that before we closed down the tape machine for the night it would be polite to ask him if he had any final words on anything that we hadn't covered. I've met a lot of rock stars, and by and large, when you say this to them, they'll say no. Paul was different. He got serious again. And if you think the discussion of the Beatles in chapter one was overblown, just listen to what Paul wanted to tell the world: "I'd like to say we're getting a reaction that no other bands are getting, a reaction that goes back to the sixties when I was going to see the Beatles. And now it's me. I think it's so great that there's a band that gives an audience so much. I think it's great that there's a band around now that can get that kind of reaction from an audience." Believe it.

I saved for last the discussion of Paul's handwriting. In a way it's almost unnecessary. Of all the members of Kiss, he is the most open, the one you can genuinely feel you know after a conversation. I think his handwriting says that quite clearly too.

It's loose and loping. It's quite wide, just as it is quite substantial on the vertical scales. It's all smooth edges, and betrays a light, friendly touch with the pen. The fact that he appends his star symbol (but not even the star is pointed) to the end of his name is not arrogant braggadocio, it's just his way of admitting without any false humility that he's proud of being a star and the "Star Lover" of the band.

All in all, Paul Stanley is a little bit macho and a little bit vain—but *always* a lover before a fighter, both in real life and in the cooperative dream world called Kiss.

Chapter 7

No Heart So Blessed:
The Simmonsiad (Long Pink)*

> That's the idea: Always a reaction, one way or
> the other.
>
> Gene Simmons, October 1976

This will not be easy.

There was a game we played in childhood called
Pin the Tail on the Donkey. It was not always
pleasant sport, because the rules required that a
player be blindfolded and then spun in circles before he was allowed to embark on his lonely and
confusing quest for the paper donkey, to which he
was to append the paper tail. To add to the player's
confusion, to his sense of being alone, to his growing sense of being a victim, there was a crowd
around him, not blindfolded, laughing and taunting
him as he dismally failed to locate the donkey and
affix his tail.

What I wish now is that we were playing Pin
the Tail on the Donkey and that each and every
reader were that blindfolded player. Such a wish
does not stem from some sadistic urge within me.
To the contrary, what I seek to do is explicate and

*Though the story of Gene Simmons is integral—even central—
to the story of Kiss, portions of this chapter contain concepts
and descriptions which might be considered profoundly repug-
nant. Reader discretion is advised.

enlighten (kindly motives if ever there were any). But it would be infinitely helpful to me in my attempt at this if you understood, even underwent, two emotional dislocations implicit in the child's game: confusion and persecution. The two concepts are intimate to the story—and the telling of the story—of Gene Simmons. . . .

You are spinning, blind, lost, and not in control, and something wet drops into your hand. One wet drop. Two. Three. Your thumb travels into the valleys of your palm, seeking some clarification of the nature of this moisture. The thumb finds the little pool and slides in, back and forth across its diameter. To your horror, the liquid is not water. It is thicker than water, and appears to adhere fairly well to itself—not to mention to you hand. The thumb dives back in. The liquid is slippery on the surface and enveloping when the thumb dips below the surface, gelatinous almost, but with a somewhat more sinewy structure. The dripping accelerates, the pool grows in you hand. Soon, the dripping is more a splatter. One splatter, quickly followed by two and three and four splatters of the slime. Globules are beginning to ricochet off your hand and strike elsewhere about your body. Suddenly, the splattering becomes a splashing, a nearly continuous torrent, and your hand drops to your side and your shoes begin to fill up. All you can do is hold your innards as the torrent continues, and hope that you stop spinning before the liquid swallows your breathing. Spinning—and the substance envelopes your knees. Spinning—and it passes your waist. Spinning—and you're chest high in the stuff, praying against the sucking force of rushing

liquid that is pulling you under, that is burglar-
izing your life. Spinning in the dark and out of
control—in the *substance*.

Of a sudden, there is a dry retching sound and
the torrent ceases. And the spinning is slowing to a
halt. *Riii-iiip!* goes the very shroud of creation.
And suddenly it is light again. You raise your
hand towards your face to check your vision, to
check your very existence—and you gasp and
choke. Your hand—your entire body, as you now
see—is covered in thick crimson plasma. You look
towards the horizon. Everywhere, plasma. A thick
red ocean, which, now receding, only covers your
knees. And the sky! The sky is pink in the reflected horror!

And then you spot him.

He is above you, almost directly, but planted
firmly on the ground next to you as you see. He is,
you reckon, forty stories high. Forty-one stories if
you count the hairball hair-knob atop his furry
skull. Behind dual black bat wings, what seems to
be a pair of eyes winks at you. He smiles, and
thirty feet of black lips stretch across his chin. It
is then that you see it. Inside the black lips, the
mouth is crimson like the plasma. From the bottom
black lip hangs a last horrid sheet of the stuff,
which drops to earth now as he runs a gigantic
tongue across his mouth. Now the chin is pink
from the residue of the substance—the substance *he*
has spewed! He smiles again. You look around, not
knowing who the gesture is intended for, and you
see that you are alone. That is, you are alone as far
as the living. Bodies float lazily past in the red
muck. And you are aghast that they are bodies you

recognize. Eric Clapton. Peter Frampton. Bad
Company. Heart. P-Funk. Hall and Oates. Good
Lord! It's Crosby, Stills and Nash. Sweet heavens
above! Ted Nugent. Aerosmith. Black Oak Arkan-
sas. Springsteen and Southside Johnny! The Band.
The Dead. The Sex Pistols. Bowie, Queen, and
Iggy! And then . . . but it can't be! And it is, and
you know it: The Beatles—John, Paul, George,
Ringo. It is moments before another corpse passes,
but you spot a lone, bulbous human remain loom-
ing into view. Closer. You don't recognize him.
Closer still. You still don't know. Suddenly, the red
current picks up one last burst of speed and sends
this last, lone corpse along downstream with the
others. You can't figure that one out, but you do
seem to remember there was a fat guy named
Elvis . . .

The voice booms startlingly from above. "Rock
'n' roll *should've* forgot," it says. You look up, but
the immense figure is gone. All around you, the
plasma has receded. It is a breathtaking spring
again. The ground is green and fruitful. You believe it is a Gypsy curse.

Like I said, this will not be easy.

What you have just been a party to (if you par-
ticipated) is the eradication of rock 'n' roll from
the face of the earth and the subsequent survival of
the true rock 'n' roll believer. The eradicator is
Gene Simmons. The survivor . . . Is it you? The
substance he spews over the earth is the red
chicken blood he spews every night on stage. It is

the chicken blood that drowns the incompetent
and insincere and restores the earth to fertile vital-
ity. Admittedly, the narrative of the story is alle-
gorical. But, make no mistake, the facts are literal.
If all those vestigial rock 'n' roll musicians don't
actually expire in Gene's nightly chicken-blood
torrent, effectively they die—their existence a use-
less appendage onto humankind.

And you are right: It *is* a Gypsy curse. Gene
Simmons's family comes from Hungary, the Gypsy
capital of the world. And Gene (born Gene Klein,
August 25, circa 1949) is the only son. Which
makes his lot a hefty one.

He carries his burden well. If Ace is the punk,
and Peter the wise old cat, and Paul the beauty
with some brains, then Gene is the smoldering
black soul of Kiss. He is the closest of the four to
totally embodying in himself the whole of what
Kiss is. Which is a helluva lot. Gene is—alternately
and simultaneously—petty and grand, grotesque
and attractive, smart and stupid, acquisitive and
magnanimous, fat and skinny, polite and rude, loving and hating, good and evil. Above all, however,
he is hellbent on tearing up the past, damning the
future, and maintaining one tarnished monument
to the existence of man on this planet: Himself.
And *that*, like it or not, is what rock 'n' roll is all
about. From Elvis shaking his fanny to the Sex Pistols sticking safety pins in their brains, rock 'n'
roll has been about loud (aurally and visually)
self-display. That's what its function has been, to
showcase loud self-display. And, in spite of all the
Peter Framptons in the world, it will go down fight-

ing, kicking, and screaming to do just that. As will Gene Simmons.

True to his stage image, Gene is probably the most maniacal of the group. You might trace this overriding characteristic of his personality back to his upbringing. For one thing he was an only child in a Brooklyn (they later moved to Queens) household with two family-oriented, doting East European parents. Now, theories of the only child abound and contradict each other on points, but the consensus maintains that lone children receive more attention and that with that attention comes an equally inordinate share of the family's expectations. The sole son (or daughter) has to be everything, accomplish everything, that a larger nest of offspring might be expected to accomplish. This makes the only child much more likely to be a perfectionist and have much higher goals for himself and push harder and longer for those goals than other children of different circumstances. The only child is extremely success-oriented. When the only child is released on the world it is reasonable to assume he will demand an inordinate amount of attention, to match that which he is used to at home.

Can anyone pick out Gene Simmons in the description above? Sure, while it's only theory, the only-child syndrome does appear to fit onto the Gene Simmons personality—at least as much as the ultracautious perfectionist will allow us to see.

Another central fact of Gene's life is that he was at one time very seriously caught up in religion. A faithful and diligent student at religious school when he was a young man, Gene considered devoting his life to religious duties. Just as with Peter Criss and Catholic school—his disillusionment with its restrictions and ultimately his fervent rebellion against *all* restrictions—Gene eventually went the other way from Yeshiva school. "I used to be very religious, but I stopped," he told *Circus* Magazine in Frank Rose's remarkably candid "Kiss Tapes" series. "I think we're here to find our own way . . . I guess I've always wanted to be God . . ." Which would just about have to sum up the concepts of parental (and otherwise) attention, religion, and rebellion in Gene Simmon's life.

So if we assume that Gene needed attention and needed to rebel (sort of reinforcing needs, one might say), how did he get the idea to effect this through Kiss? Well, it was a meandering course, but with several very strong continuous threads. As a youngster he did well in both religious and public schools. He didn't go out very much after school, preferring instead to occupy his leisure time reading comic books and watching horror movies and listening to rock 'n' roll. In school—after he had scrapped the religious plans—English probably interested him most. In comics, it was the Marvel superheroes like the Fantastic Four and Spiderman. In horror movies, it was Lon Chaney, the venerable old master of disguises, infamous as *The Hunchback of Notre Dame*. In rock 'n' roll, he is less specific, but has admitted that "that British-invasion stuff (Beatles, Stones, Yardbirds, Who, etc.) really knocked me out. All that attention lavished on those guys . . ."

As he grew up, Gene maintained his interest in English and pop culture—to the point of editing his own comic fanzines. In college at the City University of New York, he decided to major in journalism for a healthy mix of his interests. Immediately after college, he decided to try his hand at teaching—a profession more in line with his nascent bent for getting himself up in front of crowds. "I like to get up there and perform," Gene once said of his school teaching experience, at P.S. 75 in Manhattan (at Ninety-sixth Street and West End Avenue, to be precise). At night, however, he was hedging his bets by thumping away on his bass and looking around for the right rock 'n' roll band to hook up with. He continued teaching for six months, but later admitted to one reporter, "I couldn't stand the kids."

Sometime not too long after that, Gene went to work for the Xerox Corporation subsidiary, Bowker, Inc., working in the proofreading section of their *Books In Print* division. *Books In Print* is a large directory not much different from a telephone book, except that it lists titles, authors, and publishing information instead of phone numbers. In other words, reading this material day in and day out has to be a comedown for a young man with serious and rather grandiose ambitions. While the company has traditionally been a haven for between-work actors and musicians, Bowker must have lent doubts at times to Gene's theory that he was a "star."

It had to be a step up when Gene landed a job as an editorial assistant at *Vogue*—even if that meant he was little more than a glorified office boy. Still, it was clearly not what he had in mind. While he was remembered by a *Vogue* staffer as being "a fast typist and a hardworking, genial guy," he was now to enter the field where he would truly prove himself, at this point plunging headlong into the rock 'n' roll stew.

As is the case with the rest of the members of the band, Gene's past is fairly well obfuscated on purpose, in the interest of serving his and their mystique. One presumes that he didn't meet up with Paul immediately, and that he was in and out of at least a couple of groups before he landed in the one that included the kindred soul with whom he would eventually make his fortune. The important thing is, he *did* find Paul and together they did develop a concept of successful rock 'n' roll. And where do you think that concept originated? Well, it is my educated guess—Gene would never admit it—that the makeup was largely Simmons's idea, an idea he had been fascinated with all his life. Via none other than his old friends the Marvel superheroes and, especially, that leering hunchback, Lon Chaney. (Ironically, Marvel now has a Kiss comic on the stands, more on which later.) Talk about continuous threads, all that leisure time that Gene was devoting as a child to the comics and the horror shows—a devotion which just had to have been deplored by parents, no matter how doting—will be with him now the rest of his life and, in point of fact, should prove to have been the biggest single influence on his life's work. Ain't life funny?

To coin a phrase, the rest was Kisstory. And what does Gene think about his current situation? "I'm doing this," says he, "because *I* would have liked to have seen a show like this . . . and I love to have ev-

erybody looking at me. They are shouting my
name—Gene Simmons!"

While his up-front message is that he's just lapping up all the attention, what lies in the uncon-
scious speech of his handwriting?

Again, from the "Notes" of *Kiss Alive!*, we find

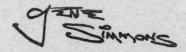

that Gene's signature is the most angular of the
group, in sharp contrast to partner Paul Stanley's
easygoing curves. Gene also has the most low-slung
signature, with most of his small letters appearing
as little more than squares. All in all, between the
rigid angularity and the vertically *and* horizontally compressed appearance of the signature, one
might speculate that Gene is the most controlled of
the group. And that while he may be soaking up a
lot of fame and glory and emotional input, he is al-
lowing very little out, the stage show aside. Sure,
he may be the most demonstrative onstage, but if
this casual look at his handwriting means anything
(and I think it does), then that is only the half of
it! Gene is a man of some deeply buried feelings.

Speaking of things that are deeply buried: Have
you ever noticed the odd dot-dash punctuation
throughout Gene's note inside *Alive!*? Have you
ever wondered if it had some sort of meaning?
Well, seeing as anything is possible, and seeing as
the punctuation is peculiar and does bear a marked
resemblance to Morse Code, I decided to check it
out in the Morse Code book to see if maybe, just

maybe Gene had a message for us. There were some very interesting results. . . .

At the end of the first paragraph of his letter is a punctuation that is traditional, three dots, sometimes called an "ellipsis." These dots would not be remarkable except for the unusual nature of the ones following in the next two paragraphs. Anyway, the three dots could either be the ellipsis of punctuation or . . . what about the S of Morse Code, represented by three dots?

OK. In the next paragraph the Morse Code connection is made more strongly several times. There is no such form of punctuation in any language that employs a dash followed immediately by three dots. The only form of communication that employs such a symbol is Morse Code. Following the word "sport" in the second paragraph of Gene's note is this dash–three-dot symbol. In the third paragraph, the symbol appears again following the words "eyes," "out," and "crazy." In Morse Code communication, this dash–three-dot symbol stands for the letter B.

Lastly, in the third and final paragraph, again, another symbol appears that has no precedent in English punctuation. The symbol is four dots. It might be a mistake with an ellipsis (which is only supposed to have three dots) but if one takes another look at the Morse Code book, one discovers that four dots is the symbol for the letter H.

What we have then if we read these Morse Code "letters" in sequence from the top of the letter to the bottom is this: S, B, B, B, B, H.

What could it stand for? Some secret Bat-Lizard code that we mere mortals cannot hope to fathom?

Speculating, you might say that the first two letters
of the sequence when turned around spell B, S—or
B.S., if you will, which stands for bull---. Is that
what Gene thinks about his note? Then, if you
turn the last two letters around, you have the initials H.B., which also happen to be the initials of a
very famous acting school. H.B. (Herbert Berg-
hoff) Studio in Manhattan. Is Gene trying to tell
us that is where he will go to school when and if he
decides to become a full-time actor—a la Lon
Chaney? Do the middle two letters, BB, stand for
BB guns? Well, it's food for thought. And you can
decide whether the elusive Bat-Lizard was attempting to throw us all off the track again with
another cryptic message. . . .

Gene Simmons, the Bat-Lizard, Denizen of Dark
Places—now you see him, now you don't. And that
seems to be just the way he wants it. I may have
his phone number in my little black book, but, for
certain, *no* one has his *number*, period. . . .

Chapter 8
Winter Comes To Hades

Where are we?
Paul Stanley, June 1974

So behind the whiteface masks of Kiss are real human beings. And within those human beings, those frail sacks of flesh, are yearnings. Call them yearnings to escape the past, yearnings to crush the past, even, and call them yearnings for a kind of love that the rest of us may only dream of, Arena Love—that emotion which renders the frailest of humans greater than the sum of their parts, that imposes on them a Place In History. Which is what we are doing now. We are bestowing Arena Love right here in these pages and carving out history.

On with it.

Therefore, in February of 1974, Casablanca released the debut album, *Kiss*, heralded that release with two successful parties, and then sat back to wait. In the meantime, the Kiss Machine hit the road with one hundred thousand dollars invested in their equipment. Did I say in Chapter 3 that it would be a long time before things would go right again? I did—and it was.

As to the album, it turned out that everybody's hope for "Kissin' Time" as a big hit single fell on deaf ears. "Kissin' Time" made barely a nick in the consciousness of the almighty radio programmers in America. Virtually nil airplay. Without a hit single it is very difficult for an album to become noticed by record consumers. *Kiss* sold very slowly. As far as the critics (who can also "break" a record or an artist if they are enthusiastic enough) were concerned, the best they could do was say the album was *all right* heavy metal, the worst they could do was to ignore it completely. While there were a few who went the former course, most took the latter. In fact, ignoring the album in print may have been the nicest thing some of the critics could have done: In private they laughed at it, and laughed again at this ridiculous costumed Alice Cooper/glitter/heavy metal retread group that had made it. It was not likely that those critics' reviews would have been anything but devastating.

As to the touring, well, even the wealthiest supergroups, who can afford their own jet planes and every conceivable mobile luxury, find life on the road just tolerable at best. Imagine the desperate plight of a new band on their first tour out, having to eschew the luxury of picking their gigs, and playing instead any date opening for any group that would have them. Did you say hell? Hell is not a strong enough word. From March through July of '74, Kiss played every tank town between New York and Los Angeles—and then some—opening for some groups that were never heard from again.

Case in point, I had my first personal encounter with the band as early as May of '74. At the time

I was living in San Francisco, and the band was passing through. An editor phoned me about doing a story on a band that no one had hardly heard of, a glitter band, he said, called Kiss. I agreed, got in touch with Casablanca, and arranged to do the article. By May they had been on the road several months, but down at the hotel where the interview took place they still appeared enthusiastic and the road giddies were only in their very earliest stages. Paul arrived at our appointment from another section of the city where he had just been on the receiving end of the famed tattooist (he also did Janis Joplin) Lyle Tuttle's arcane art. In other words, he arrived in the room with a brand new—and very sore—tattoo of a rose affixed to his shoulder. A fact which I interpret as the beginning of the road crazies.

And why shouldn't they be crazy? Who were they scheduled to open for at San Francisco's notorious psychedelic artifact, Winterland, that night? Why, none other than Savoy Brown. Who? That's right: Savoy Brown, a blues band that may have been around since the dawn of creation (perhaps 1966) whose featured player/founder was blues-flash guitarist Kim Simmonds. At one time, Savoy Brown had been fairly popular, even teetering on the brink of true stardom, but by 1974 ... well, *you* don't remember them, do you? So Kiss was opening for Savoy Brown (and they received a small but very enthusiastic reception for their set), which is one thing. But after San Francisco, Kiss was headed for a concert in Alaska, which is another thing entirely. (They happen to have been the last "name" rock group to have played in the

snowy beyond right up till the present.) As the
touring wore on into June and July, averaging fifteen one-night stands per month, I assure you they
were getting nuts, despite the fact that their small
audiences reacted favorably. Peter allegedly re-
marked at the time: "If we don't get rich from
this, they're going to have to put me in a padded
celll." So there.

By August of '74 it was abundantly clear to everyone that Richard Nixon had to resign or be im-
peached from the presidency. By August of '74 it
was also abundantly clear that their first album, in
spite of the similarities in cover photos, would not
be Kiss's *Meet the Beatles* and that "Kissin' Time"
had failed to become their "I Want To Hold
Your Hand." Indeed, Nixon resigned, Jerry Ford
tripped into office, and Kiss entered a recording
studio for the second time.

Once again the band signed up Kenny Kerner
and Richie Wise to produce, but this time they
decided to give recording a try in Los Angeles,
where they might be closer to the head office of
Casablanca. While one recording studio is not
much different from another (unless of course it's
one of those home jobbies that superstars are in-
stalling these days), and physically Village Recorder in L.A. is only a bit plusher than Bell Sound
Studios in New York City, New York is the
band's home and spiritual base. So it's reasonable to
speculate that Kiss may have been homesick. Then
again, they may have been exhausted from the
endless months on the road. Whatever it was, the
songwriting for these recording sessions seemed to
have backslid somewhat, and the end result failed

to match up to their stunning—albeit overlooked—debut LP. On the other hand, *Hotter Than Hell* was also a more ambitious project all round.

If you don't notice as soon as the first cut that Kiss is up to bigger things, then you just aren't paying attention. "Got to Choose," the LP's best tune, sounds something like the Stones (circa "Jumpin' Jack Flash") crossed with Grand Funk (circa "We're an American Band") and Ike and Tina Turner's Ikettes. Needless to say, it's a hairy and aggressive animal, this song that charges out of your speakers in a dazzling zigzag pattern, leaving you utterly confused and in awe as it sweeps past to give Ace the touchdown in one of his most remarkable solos. For starters, I might explain that Kiss knows how to open a record album ("Strutter" opened the first one), and here they come out with full-blown soul vocals that sound like nothing on *Kiss*. Not only is the background harmonizing louder than before, but it's richer—with a warbling top end to it that would do any soul group proud. Add to that the customary gutter vibrations of the bass guitar's metal onslaught and you have a pretty spectacular hybrid. Then comes Ace. Once every album he seems to crank it up to full steam; two, maybe three times he may have shut down the rest of the rock 'n' roll guitarists when he does this: "Got to Choose" is Ace at full steam, knocking 'em down. Sacrificing none of the base, visceral feel, Ace travels through a long sequence of notes that is so complex it surely must be ranked as his greatest solo composition. While it sounds at first like Ace just tearing away, he surprises halfway into his spot by seeming to modulate (that is, change keys)

up. As you wait for the band to take off with him,
you realize that he has performed a *trompe l'oreille*,
a trick, whereby he *sounds* like he is modulating
but he is actually just playing a few wrong notes
intentionally. That's exciting, and jacks up the action of the song several notches. But wait. When, a
full eight bars later, he does it *again*, there's nothing to do but fall over dead, slain by wonderful
rock 'n' roll. "Got to Choose" is *the* song on the
LP, and, for Ace-watchers, one to study in the eons
to come (it would take that long to figure the damn
thing out!).

The pace begins to slow on the next cut, "Para-
site," in spite of the hyped-up classic Yardbirds'
riff that holds the song together. But when "Goin'
Blind" hits the stylus, the pace stops. "Goin' Blind"
is the band's very first (and last, for a while) ballad. Written and sung by Gene it is electric,
unlike the next ballad they will do, "Beth," and
it concerns itself with a great degree of pain, de-
tailing the story of a man who says he's ninety-
three, attempting to communicate (in one way or
another) with a sixteen-year-old nymphet. It is
much in the same vein as *Songs For A Tailor*, a
set of songs by another great bassist, Jack Bruce
of the heavy-metal founding fathers' group, Cream.
Like Bruce's set, it is beautiful in a way, but too
depressing both in lyrics and mournful musical
dronings to be fully accessible. Interesting because
Gene is pained—uninteresting because he is painful. It is not surprising that slow songs were
shelved for several albums after this.

"Hotter Than Hell" picks things up after that,
but seems at times to be rote heavy metal, copping

Eric Clapton's too-well-known "Layla" guitar figure. "Let Me Go, Rock 'n' Roll" is the one that sal-
vages everything. Like the first song on the side,
"Let Me Go" has a greater vocal depth than Kiss
had previously demonstrated. However, this time
the vocals seem better integrated into the band's
style as well as into the song. It is perhaps the most
upbeat and catchy tune of the second LP, and undoubtedly the band knew it. Listen carefully and
you will see the foundations for their first big hit,
"Rock and Roll All Nite." Note especially the
melody of the chorus, the drum segue from verse to
verse, and Ace's solo, which starts off almost identically to the staccato sizzler on that hit. "Let
Me Go, Rock 'n' Roll" is the LP's other *great* cut.

As was the case with the first album, side two of
Hotter Than Hell falls down from the high of side
one. Apparently the band was still insecure enough
(justifiably, maybe) to shoot their shot on the first
side, thinking that that might be the only chance
they got with a lot of very casual listeners. The
opening cut on side two is more-sparse heavy metal,
inspired by the Stones' devilishly empty "Honky
Tonk Women." It is a decent song, well-played,
but seems nearly unnecessary after side one's "Got
to Choose."

Cut two, side two is the kicker. Coming on with
a solid Cream-inspired cold-steel riff, Gene regales
us with the ultimate paranoia song, finally warning
the confused female character in the song that everybody is watching her. Listening to this song,
more than any other, one might imagine Gene *not*
a person to be stoned with. "Watchin' You," therefore, is a perfect evocation of Gene as the Bat-Liz-

ard Monster. "Mainline," which follows, and
which is not about drugs, but about getting a hit
of love, is just a good ole rock 'n' roll song in the
Chuck Berry tradition, as is "Comin' Home,"
which follows that.

One wonders if the homesick lyrics to "Comin'
Home" actually betray the aforementioned home-
sickness or are just another song about the road.
I prefer to think the former, though it should
be noted that this is the first Kiss song that is
at least partially about touring in a band. The album's final cut, "Strange Ways," is a return to
monolithic metallic bombast, but is most in-
triguing because of the vocal. At first, it's very
hard to tell who is actually singing: The voice is
young, smooth, and capable of a very consistent
and attractive vibrato. When the singer sails into a
scream, there's no question but that it's Peter at
work. "Strange Ways" is, indeed, a strange and
one-time-only vocal performance from the Star-
lover, and his fans should know it.

The best cuts from this album were rerecorded
live for *Alive!*, but the LP has merit in revealing
the experiments both failed and successful that
went into the later Kiss breakthrough. And the
cover is a story in itself. Briefly, the cover of *Hotter Than Hell* includes a translation into Japanese
of titles and names. The idea being that the huge
Japanese record market might be ready for Kiss before America, and might be enticed by the band's
graciously bilingual cover copy (they were, to a
remarkable extent). Further, the cover reveals that
Peter has altered his makeup from the first album,
removing the admittedly extraneous red extension

to his Kitty whiskers, as well as the ill-conceived red goatee from under his lip. Lastly, if you do a comparison you will note that while Kiss may have been influenced by the Beatles' first album photo on their own first album, the Beatles turned the tables, and on their *Rock 'n' Roll Music* greatest hits collection of late '76 were influenced by Kiss—the same hands are shown holding the jacket on both records!

Anyway, the band had completed the album by the end of September '74, and a lot of hopes were riding on it. It was released on October 22, but there were no parties *this* time. Kiss was already back grinding it out on the road.

Chapter 9
The Snowball's Last Chance

Where are we?
Paul Stanley, January 1975

They toured. And then they toured some more. There's that old expression, used in reference to people that are doomed, they say that those people have a snowball's chance in hell. In the Kiss saga, at this point in late '74, they had a snowball's chance in *Hotter Than Hell* (which, one might deduce, is even less of a chance).

The album was selling a little better than the debut LP, particularly where the band played concerts (and played them again), but that wasn't saying much, especially considering the money invested in hydraulic lifts for Peter's drums, huge lighted Kiss logo signs, and mounds of musical equipment. Japan seemed pleased, as intended, but how the hell were they ever going to get to Japan at this rate? *Hotter Than Hell* needed airplay in order that mass numbers of people might become aware of it—the LP wasn't getting any at all. The folks at Casablanca waited this time to see if the radio stations would pick up on one cut that they could then release as a single—nothing. So the band continued to hit the boards.

While such a touring routine and such disappointing record sales might have terminally discouraged others, Kiss seemed to be doing quite well, even hitting their stride in concert performance. And getting great reactions back. Slowly, the crowds that turned out at shows were getting bigger and more vocal for the opening act, Kiss, as the word of mouth went out about this bizarre and manic new group. Where the record execs were looking at the LP sales figures, the band was bolstered by what they were seeing out in the rock 'n' roll trenches. They had gotten over their naïve belief that stardom might happen overnight, but they became confident that it would only be a matter of time and lots of hard work. They were willing. Then something happened that they might have sniffed in the air, but never *really* expected.

The headline acts, seeing the response to the opening band and the concomitant diminished response to their own set, started to balk at having a group so outrageous billed with them. They complained about the ridiculous makeup and the flashpots and the sign and the fire-breathing, and the teeny-bopperish appeal of the whole thing. They considered themselves above this. What they didn't admit was that they were jealous and that Kiss was stealing their thunder.

Soon Aucoin was getting turned down when he attempted to book tours for Kiss accompanying other groups. Trouble. The band might suddenly find themselves in Wichita with no place to go but home. With neither of the first two albums burning up the record charts, this would not do. Kiss had to be out there in front of the public; their live show was the most persuasive promotional instrument, the most effective way they could attract record buyers. Aucoin scrambled for anything he could get the band. But the fear of Kiss was spreading through the hearts of wasting rock 'n' roll bands throughout the land, and the gigs were becoming scarcer.

One gig they did land was back in New York City, home, at the Academy of Music on Fourteenth Street (now the Palladium) on New Year's Eve, 1974. It would not be a gig any of the players or the spectators would forget for a long time. The entire bill was heavy-metal heaven, featuring Kiss, as well as the legendary Iggy and the Stooges, and headlining the nightmarishly delightful Blue Oyster Cult plus some surprises.

Seeing as their luck had not been running high, the N.Y.C. gig would be a special event—a homecoming—and a boost to morale. In order to dramatize and crystallize the situation in the minds of his associates, Gene pulled a surprise. They weren't just going to straggle into the infamous Academy under their own steam, he would hire them a limousine! Without breathing a word of it, Gene casually insisted that he pick everyone up before the show. When he arrived in the long black Cadillac with chauffeur, it was all any of them could do to keep from blowing the cool that such an automobile called for. They were still just journeyman rock musicians at this point, not rock stars, but damn it if they weren't going to feel like they were the genuine item tonight! They were bursting with pride. After the trip and their grand arrival at the hall, echoing Brando's *On the Water-*

front words, Peter supposedly told a bystander:
"In that car I felt like I wasn't just anybody, I
was *somebody*!" Gene's surprise was a huge
success. Needless to say, they took the stage in high
spirits that night.

And take the stage they did! Kiss came on like a
ball of fire, literally. Within minutes into their
opening number, "Deuce," the band had galva-
nized the audience, none of whom had been able to
see them perform since the relatively Neanderthal
days at the Hotel Diplomat. The fans were en-
thralled, their eyes riveted to the strange figures
onstage as they bounced up and down to the music,
oblivious of the cheap New Year's Eve wine slosh-
ing around in their bellies. The many critics in
the audience were dumbstruck and could only
scratch their heads nostalgically for the days when
rock 'n' roll was something else—something that
was safe, though they refused to acknowledge that
fact.

Midway through their powerhouse set, Gene
pulled another surprise. He is standing stage front
brandishing the torch with which he will exhale
fire. He leans back, and into the torch, taking the
flame in his coated mouth, when all of a sudden as
he leans forward to expel the fireball, a roadie from
backstage gasps. Gene doesn't notice and spews his
fire, turning back to the torch for another round
when he is enveloped by the eagle-eyed roadie,
who douses the torch, throws a towel over Gene's
head and starts to pummel it. *Gene has lit his hair
on fire!* Within a moment, the fire is out—the
roadie's alert thinking saved most of the Bat-Lizard's mane and, more than that, maybe his life.

Gene is grateful and only slightly shook. The song continues. The audience is completely knocked out—*they* think the whole incident is part of the show! From that moment till the close of their set, Kiss could do no wrong for this crowd.

Backstage afterwards, people dash into the band's dressing room to inquire after Gene's health. Two of those inquiring are Todd Rundgren and Rick Derringer, who after being assured that Gene is OK, sit down to admonish him against playing with fire in the future and to admit that they enjoyed the show. The band lights up (no pun): It is nearly the first acceptance they have gotten from their peers in the music biz. Back outside in the hall, the audience is treated to the outrageous spectacle of Iggy, the man who has cut himself with glass during his show, trying to outdo Kiss. Still later, the Cult marches on and to augment their show, brings over the oom-pah band from the famous German restaurant, Luchow's, next door to the Academy, to play an oddball version of "Auld Lang Syne."

In other words, on New Year's Eve, 1974, you hadda have been there! A wild night and a triumphant mini-homecoming (a real one must come still later) for Kiss . . . Even if they are billed below an oom-pah band in Tyrolean hats!

Well, the band had their night of cheer, and now the business of becoming stars, of becoming what they know themselves to be, must go forward. They head back out on the road, wherever they can go.

It was becoming clear to Casablanca that they would have to indicate to the world the choice of

single from the *Hotter Than Hell* album; radio
programmers were just not catching on. On January 10, 1975, Casablanca made the wise move of releasing a single version of "Let Me Go, Rock 'n'
Roll." (In the official history of the band, this
record is listed as the first single release ever by
Kiss, conveniently—or maybe just absentmindedly—forgetting "Kissin' Time.") The single did
not shoot up the charts, failed in fact to generate
any serious enthusiasm or airplay. Thus: No surge
in LP sales. Casablanca and Aucoin, both of whom
were yet to realize any profit from this expensive
venture, decided with the band that it was time to
go into the studio and try again.

Dropping Kerner and Wise, the three factions
elected Casablanca chief Neil Bogart to produce the
new album, and again Kiss would record in Los
Angeles. One month after their New York success,
the band enters the studio. Hoping.

In sum, what they came up with this time was
stronger than *Hotter Than Hell*, not as consistent
as *Kiss*, but at its high points it cut both of them.

The prime strength of *Dressed to Kill*? The album contains the first recording of the greatest
rock 'n' roll song of all time (is that enough for
ya?)—namely, "Rock and Roll All Nite." And if
they had never done anything after it, the song
would be reason enough for everyone to get down
on their knees and face Los Angeles once a day and
thank the god of smog and thunder for the rock
group Kiss and the recording session that day.

"Rock and Roll All Nite" is a classic rock 'n'
roll anthem, and at the time of its release there
hadn't been one since the heyday in '64–'66 of the

Beatles and the Stones. It was, and *is*, the anthem of the '70s. It has the kind of rousing Universal Rebel lyrics that people are moved to paint on signs and scrawl on bathroom walls. Yes, rock and roll all nite, yes, that *is* what we *really* want to do! Combine such words with a melody that defies sleep and the umpteenth playing of a McDonald's jingle, a melody that won't be displaced from its rapturous victim's head, and you have yourself a powerful chunk of rock 'n' roll. As a matter of fact, you have the reason that rock 'n' roll was born! Unbelievably, the band did it even better at a later date and with another producer (I'm getting to that one very soon)—but don't you always remember the *first* time?

There are a few more gems on the album, but nothing to compare to the carat weight and clarity of "Rock." "Room Service" is sleazy in the finest Kiss tradition, and their first *blatant* and complete road song (you can see the road is becoming part of them), and "C'mon and Love Me" by Paul is a sizzling pleader and his most sophisticated tune till then. The twelve-string guitar intro by Ace to "Rock Bottom" is the first extended experiment by the band with acoustic instruments, and is interesting as history because in it one can readily detect the ideas that will blossom on *Destroyer* and on parts of *Rock And Roll Over*. That aside, however, the song is disappointing.

As to the rest of the disk, it would be nigh on blasphemous to mention lesser (though not bad) songs in the same breath as "Rock and Roll All Nite." Oddly enough, on this album for the first time, side two seems the stronger side, containing both "Rock" and "C'mon."

The cover to *Dressed* does deserve special mention, as it is the first and only time the public has ever seen Kiss in street clothes. The cover photo was shot on the southwest corner of the Twenty-third Street and Eighth Avenue intersection in Manhattan (very near the group's first rehearsal loft).

Dressed To Kill was released on March 19, 1975 (for those of you who keep track of national holidays) and, as before, the band was back on tour. On April 2, Casablanca released the first single from the LP, the sure-to-win "Rock and Roll All Nite." Still no airplay. Still no mass sales, though the new LP sells better than ever and Kiss concerts are becoming minor events. Casablanca is floundering financially, taking another drubbing with a bomb album of greatest moments from Johnny Carson's *Tonight Show*. The company teeters on the brink and is reportedly unable to pay Kiss even the meager royalties (relatively speaking) they have earned from their records.

Out on the road, Aucoin and the band see their ground swell of support picking up. The band begins to headline at certain venues. It is clearly no time to go out of business. In a dramatic and dangerous move, Aucoin, whose resources are likewise drying up fast, decides to see how far they can get financing the latest tour with his American Express card. . . .

The tragedy of it all: The greatest rock 'n' roll song ever penned is out there and available to the public on Kiss's *Dressed To Kill*, and the public is

just not taking advantage of their good fortune!
For Kiss, in the spring of '75, it was truly the best
of times and the very worst of times. And something had to give.

SIDE TWO

Chapter 10
Hot Snowballs Redux

Alive! is what we stand for. That album *is* rock 'n' roll.

Paul Stanley, October 1976

And give it did. Kiss had released three singles, three albums, and had been on the road for over fifteen months, in the late spring of '75, when all of a sudden Detroit went insane. Long a haven for great late-breaking heavy rock 'n' rollers—such as Bob Seger, Iggy and the Stooges, Grand Funk, Ted Nugent, and the MC5—Detroit took to Kiss like arsonists to a burning skyscraper. By early May, the city was selling out *Dressed To Kill*, had put their favorite cut, "C'mon and Love Me," onto radio playlists (as an LP cut, no less) and the city's only national rock mag *Creem* was planning a major feature on the group that was taking the Motor City by firestorm. The Detroit reports were coming fast and furious to Aucoin and the band, out on tour in the even more remote hinterlands, and they lost no time.

They decided to book Detroit's massive Cobo Hall for a night in late May, and crossed their fingers. Within a matter of days, the date had sold out. Their biggest coup yet, it was clear that Kiss had arrived as a concert attraction. From here on

in it would be strictly headline status for Gotham's
masked quartet. Thrilled by the Cobo sell-out, Aucoin, Casablanca, and the band decided that maybe
it was time to collect all the best songs from the
first three albums into one explosive live set. It
was becoming increasingly clear that live was
where Kiss was most effective. To that end, the
boys contacted their old friend, Electric Lady
Studio producer Eddie Kramer, and requested him
to fly in and record the Detroit show. Kramer
obliged.

The Detroit show was a smash, and radio in the
area was jumping all over the records. Kramer had
a solid recording. The band traveled on, and
Kramer rejoined then for selected dates with
recording facilities, capturing further live performances. By July 10, Casablanca had to give in to
the will of the people, and "C'mon and Love Me"
was released as a single, subsequently becoming
Kiss's first minor hit nationally. In August, Kiss
and Kramer, satisfied with the selection of live
recordings, headed back to New York City to mix
an album from the tapes at Electric Lady Studios.
By late August they had created a master tape
recording that they believed was nothing less than
earth-shattering. The fact was that it *had* to be. For
no matter how well they were doing in concert
(and by now they were selling out consistently),
they had to have a record to really make back their
money.

On September 10, 1975, Casablanca Records released a double-LP set, recorded live by Eddie
Kramer. It was called *Kiss Alive!*

Earth-shattering is not the word.

Kiss Alive! has to rank on any true rockophile's list of the top albums of all time, and certainly at the head of any list of live recordings. It is a masterpiece.

Alive!, first of all, contains all the best songs from the first three albums, "Strutter," "Nothin' To Lose," "Firehouse," "Cold Gin," "Deuce," "Got to Choose," "Let Me Go, Rock 'n' Roll." "C'mon and Love Me," "Black Diamond," and, of course, "Rock and Roll All Nite"—a veritable greatest-hits collection. (Not that the rest of the songs are slop either!) And performed live, each one of these inherently powerful pieces of rock 'n' roll is literally transformed, synergized into something vastly greater yet—which is some monstrous feat.

Second of all, the performances of each player on *Alive!* are nonpareil. Plus, one gets Kiss in a spontaneous situation in a highly charged auditorium atmosphere—a combination that is hard to beat for exciting surprises and raw, unbridled emotion. For God's sake, here in this hall is that which they live for: Arena Love! And if you don't think they're going to completely knock themselves out to get it, you haven't been reading this book.

Thirdly, it is and will be evermore to the credit of console genius Eddie Kramer, who produced and engineered these recordings, that the Kiss Concert Experience was ever pressed into two compact slabs of vinyl. In fact, it's almost a miracle. Yet he did it, and the production sacrifices nothing to the technology of recording: bass vibrations still throttle your sphincter muscles, the midrange rhythm sounds still build little brick houses in your ears, and Ace's solos still tear those little houses down. Full-bodied, clear, both at the low and high ends, this production has to be one of the finest ever on a live record.

But the core of the *Alive!* set, the grisly, purple throbbing center of the experience of this album is the ultimate rock 'n' roll song of all time. I'm talking about "Rock and Roll All Nite" (nods head reverentially).

Alive!'s "Rock and Roll All Nite" is a radical refurbishing and fleshing out of the raw material originally recorded in the studio. "Rock and Roll All Nite" on *Alive!* is the definitive version, the way the song should always be.

What is immediately evident is the drums . . .

Dumpump-chucka, dumpump-chucka. Did you ever see *2001: A Space Odyssey?* Dumpump-chucka, dumpump-chucka. Well, in the film (directed by Stanley Kubrick), Keir Dullea plays the role of an astronaut stationed on an orbiting space station run by a supersophisticated computer named HAL, a computer which is capable of a wide range of human emotions in addition to its intellectual prowess. Dumpump-chucka, dumpump-chucka. Just like any self-respecting businessman or scientist (or writer) in this high-tech, high-pressured modern society, HAL eventually feels the strain and begins to drop a few of his screws. Dumpump-chucka, dumpump-chucka. And just like any self-respecting organization in modern society, the space station's human powers-that-be decide it's about time to ease ol' HAL out of the picture. Dumpump-chucka. Possessing a range of human-type emotions and perceptual capacities, HAL recognizes the newly conspiratorial atmosphere congealing about him at the space station, and in an effort to salvage his dignity, begins to fight back, begins to seek revenge. Dumpump-chucka, dumpump-chucka. Dumpump-chucka, dumpump-chucka. The upshot of HAL's scheming is that all the crew is killed off except Keir Dullea, who is fortunately able to destroy HAL (and the station simultaneously) and escape to a space-transport vehicle. Dumpump-chucka, dumpump-chucka. For some reason, Dullea is then forced to travel far out into space. Dumpump-chucka, dumpump-chucka. He goes beyond charted systems and in and out of time-warp zones, accelerating all the while. Dumpump-chucka, dumpump-chucka. Dumpump-chucka-dumpump-chucka. Finally, he is traveling so fast that he is no longer located on any geometric plane, but is, instead, rocketing down a neon corridor *between* planes. Dumpump-chucka-dumpump-chucka. First, he is vertical. Dumpump-chucka-dumpumpchucka. Then, he is horizontal. Dumpumpchucka-dumpumpchucka. Very, very fast. Dumpumpchuckadumpumpchucka. Until the neon corridors are a shocking and barely discernible haze on all sides. Dumpumpchucka-dumdumpchuckadumpumpchucka. And man melds into space. Dumpumpchuckadumpumpchucka. And man melds into time. Dumpumpchuckadumpumpchucka. And man becomes his past and his future, dumpumpchucka dumpump, and is revealed to himself both as man, dumpumpchucka-dumpump, and · fetus-dumpumpchucka-cascading together-dumpumpchucka-through eternity-dumpumpchuckadumpumpchuckadumpumpchucka - dumpumpchuckadumpump—Until. Suddenly. All. Stops.

And Keir Dullea stands in a bright, white fluorescent bedroom confronting the banal.

But *you* aren't. *You* don't have to . . .

The auditorium lights flash on. Dumpump-chucka-dumpump-chucka. Fluorescent lights. Dumpump-chucka-dumpump-chucka. Dumpump-chucka, dumpump-chucka—Until, suddenly the power chords strike six times, shattering the beat, devastating the fluorescence: *Pow! Pow! Pow! Pow! Powpow!*

And you crane your head out from under twenty thousand misread aspirations and, eyes aglow, whisper, "Yes!" to Paul's imploring. "Yes! . . ." Screaming: "OY WANNA ROK UN ROWL AWL NOYT UN PAWDEE EV-VARY DEH!!!!!!"

And all is peace—in the chaos of the soul's frenetic four-quarter motion.

On October 14, 1975, Casablanca Records of Los Angeles, California, U.S.A., Planet Earth, released the ultimate rock 'n' roll single from the ultimate rock 'n' roll album. Within a short time, the live "Rock and Roll All Nite" had become the first certifiable AM/FM radio smash hit for the unbelievable rock group Kiss. Victory. The forces of bleakness vanquished by the forces of black. True rock 'n' roll lives. By November of that same year, the album from which the single has been culled, *Kiss Alive!*, is certified by the Recording Industry Association of America as a gold record for sales in excess of a half-million dollars. On the road, the rock group Kiss is repeatedly called upon to headline concerts at the most prominent venues. They accept. The crowds at those venues lose their marbles. In Terre Haute, Indiana, a crusading Kiss fan, who had led a demonstration against his local radio station, dubs his band of believers the Kiss Army. Again in November, Kiss jets to Terre Haute to salute these intrepid souls on the first official Kiss Day.

In November of '75 it is clear: The rock group Kiss has *arrived*.

Chapter 11
A Touch of Classy

I like champagne.
                Ace Frehley, June 1975

How can you tell if you have a hit single? Well, first of all, you can look at the record charts in music-biz trade papers like *Billboard* and *Record World*. Secondly, you can listen to the radio. Another way might be to check your bank account. Then again, if you've really got a monster on your hands, you can just walk down the street . . . Had any member of Kiss been with me one pleasant afternoon in November of 1975 as I strolled down Twelfth Street in Manhattan, he would have known immediately what the score was: There on the corner near Sixth Avenue, three young teenagers crowded together on the trunk of a parked car. As I passed, I could hear that they were singing and could make out just the last half of a verse. ". . . and party *every* day," they intoned. Surely, I knew then, Kiss was riding a monster hit record. Something that would be very hard to top.

And top it they wouldn't. I explain:

Kiss had completely hewed to the rock 'n' roll line throughout their career. Two very long years and four albums of the hardest, loudest, most elemental music in the world. And, oh Lord, did they know it when they were out on the road! What they really needed, as '75 wound to a close, was a break, time to replenish the raw emotions they so cavalierly expended night after night whether onstage or in the studio. Perhaps they also believed their audience needed a rest, a change of pace. Perhaps also they feared the success of *Alive!* and "Rock and Roll All Nite," wondering if they could ever possibly do it again.

But after working so long and furiously, Kiss was not going to just slip away beneath the nation's consciousness. Nossir! So a vacation was out of the question. They must record a new LP. They must keep that patented Kiss vinyl out there in front of eager consumers. But, as Paul emphasized to me: "After three or four albums you want to try something a little different." The Kiss team went into a huddle.

What emerged from that huddle was an idea for an LP that would not try to top *Alive!*, but rather would take Kiss's music on a different tack. The record would be called *Destroyer*, and on it, as the title implied, a lot of what had gone before would be laid to waste. Kiss had also hit on the perfect producer, Bob Ezrin (of Alice Cooper fame). Not a man who is often contented to just sit behind a console, Ezrin is more likely to become almost another member of the band, contributing major ideas about arranging, as well as writing songs and working out on an instrument. Kiss knew that an album produced by Ezrin would be more a Kiss-Ezrin record than the pure thing. And that's just what they wanted: new input. In addition to

Ezrin, to further agitate the mix, to jumble the deck, Kiss decided to call in veteran L.A. manager/songwriter/producer/rockmaniac Kim Fowley to co-pen some tunes. Sure! That'll be just great! Tear up the rule book and throw it away! After all, what they have in mind is a real *Destroyer*. The entire crew entered New York City's Record Plant in December of '75. It would be the longest stint ever in the studio for Kiss, and, in the end, they got just what they had come for.

But wait. One last thing had to be taken care of as they greeted the New Year. It had been nearly a year since Kiss had performed at the infamous Academy of Music New Year's Eve show in New York. In fact, that had been the last time they had played their home town. Weren't they entitled to soak up a little praise from the home boys now that they had returned to the city as stars? Of course. And to that end, Aucoin booked them into Long Island's huge Nassau Coliseum for New Year's Eve '75. Taking a break in the intense but thoroughly enjoyable songwriting and recording activities at the Record Plant, the band traveled the forty-five minutes to the Coliseum to play their victory show. The place was sold out, and the crowd devoured every last moment of Kiss fire-and-lightning performance. Their families and friends from all over the metropolitan area clapped them on the back in total approval and beamed with pride. But beyond that, Kiss may have enjoyed a bit of sweet revenge that evening. Who was the opening act this chilly Long Island night? None other than the Blue Oyster Cult. My, how a year can turn things around . . .

Settled back down to business in the studio, Kiss
found that they were getting just the change they
had been seeking. There were ideas floating around
and things going on in these sessions that they had
never been involved with before. New combina-
tions of songwriters were being formed at every
turn. The sessions, under the firmly guiding hand
of Ezrin, the pro's pro, became more like a pleasur-
able working vacation than a lazy respite, and the
boys were learning a lot.

In the outside world, perhaps fueled by a mis-
chievous publicity department at Rock Steady, the
weird rumors were flying. Among the rock press,
the word was about that Kiss, the nation's number
one down-and-dirty heavy metal band, was hauling
a boys' choir from some church into their studio at
the Record Plant. Boys' choirs? *Church?* Yeah, and
not only that, went the rumors, but they got string
quartets and grand pianos and tubular bells up
there, too! "Gads?" came the press's response. But
there's more, the rumors flew back again. This new
one is gonna have synthesizers and all kinds of
electronic effects! While the rock writers drew
their breaths and bemoaned the deterioration of
true rock 'n' roll, they dutifully reported what they
were hearing, and by the time the rumors had gone
through seventeen hands, twenty-seven rewrites
and retellings, Kiss had become Emerson, Lake,
and Palmer in whiteface plundering the Vienna
Boys' Choir with space guns while whistling Gre-
gorian Chants in 7/4 time. Some of the fans were
becoming understandably perturbed at the expected spectacle.

On March 1, 1976, those fans were relieved to

hear the preview single released by Casablanca.
"Shout It Out Loud" was, for sure, the slickest
recording ever by the band, but aside from the
grand piano, it wasn't much more than a polished
rocker in the "Rock and Roll All Nite" vein.
Phew! Happily, radio programmers began spinning the new disc, and Kiss fans all over America
were back in the groove.

Then, on March 15, Casablanca dropped the
bombshell. *Destroyer*, the album, was released *in
toto*. Besides the grand piano of "Shout," this LP
included a host of sounds not previously heard
from Kiss. These included: a synthesizer, tubular
bells, a string quartet, some electronic effects,
and—horror of all horrors!—a boys' church choir!
On first listen, many fans couldn't believe their
ears. Had Kiss really gone ELP with space guns,
church, and ancient melodies? By their second listen, in spite of themselves perhaps, fans were
warming to the album. By third and fourth hear-
ings, they were back in love—it was Kiss all along,
they realized. Within a month, *Destroyer* became
the band's second gold album. (In the meantime,
during the sessions, *Alive!* had been certified platinum by the R.I.A.A., for sales in excess of a million
units!)

It's not hard to see how Kiss afficionados were
confused and maybe a bit put off by *Destroyer* at
first. Even Paul has admitted that "*Destroyer* was an
excursion for us, an experiment of sorts to try and
do something a little different. For my money, it's
a great album. I enjoy it a lot—but it's not a true,
full-bodied Kiss album." Indeed.

Side one leads right off with the only electronic

musique-concréte-type event that Kiss has ever put
onto a record. While it's not weird at all, as far as
those things go, being simply the sounds of somebody eating a meal, walking out of a house, starting a car, and driving away while fiddling with
the radio dial, it is a departure for the group. In
fact, the contrast between this record and others is
all the more starkly drawn when the car radio starts
to play an excerpt from Kiss's masterful hard-rock
anthem, "Rock and Roll All Nite." The song that
follows all this, however, should not disturb any
fan. "Detroit, Rock City" (commemorating the
town that finally broke the band big) is in the classic Kiss tradition of sparse and pounding bass-
drums tunes, and the lyrics, as anarchic and
partyized as anything the band has ever cut. The
next cut, "King of the Night Time World," may
not be as strong, but, likewise, except for high-
gloss production, it contains as little extraneous
matter as any of the group's previous efforts—reports that Frank Sinatra is planning to cover it on
his next record aside. And what's all the fuss about
Paul's song for Gene, "God of Thunder"? Again,
discounting what might be just increased profes-
sionalism in recording, the song is similar to any
of a number of the monster's thumpamatic incanta-
tions, "Nothin' To Lose," to mention one.

But, aha! Here's the rub: "Great Expectations."
It starts off all right with Gene beckoning lasciviously and suggesting that he knows of his fans'
desires for his mouth and what it could do for
them; but then two or three choruses in, these tubular bells begin to play along with the hookline
melody and—what's that high-pitched noise? Yes,

fans, that *is* the darkly rumored boys' choir itself, singing right along. But in the end, isn't it merely an interesting counterpoint, an ironic twist, and an *enhancement* to the patently lurid lyrics the Bat-Lizard is spewing?

Side two kicks off—again, fully oiled with high-class production—tough and ready to rumble with the band's second greatest teen-age anthem, "Flaming Youth." What is surprising about this song is not that the calliopelike organ embellishment may have turned some folks off, but that the song didn't inspire the Revolution. Gene goes down in the gutter again for the next song, and the only thing he comes up with that is not absolutely rock bottom Kiss sleaze is a rhythm guitar that sounds like it's played through a distorting Leslie amplifier. "Shout It Out Loud," which follows that, has already been dissected and approved for party use. The side and the album ends with "Do You Love Me," which busts out of the gate with some trash-can drumming that is vintage Dave Clark Five (they were the real prophets of heavy metal back in '64 and the first band to knock the Beatles out of the number one slot on the British charts) and classic rock 'n' roll in any arena. And that's pretty much the sum total of *Destroyer*: Kiss rock 'n' roll with just a touch of class.

If you think I've forgotten a tune, you're wrong. Purposefully, I have left discussion of Peter Criss's "Beth" till last. Because not only is this soapy symphonic ballad the kink in the album, it is also the Big Connection.

"Beth" put Kiss over commercially in markets they may never have dreamed of cracking. Specifically, while the band seemed to have captivated the rock-arena crowd with the scintillating live show and the blockbuster rabble rouser "Rock and Roll All Nite," "Beth," due to the efforts of some very sharp Kiss Army soldiers, snuck them onto MOR (middle of the road) radio and subsequently into the hearts of MOR's main listeners, the over-thirties.

The appeal of this song is readily apparent. Even the most diehard metallic drones amongst us must find it hard to keep the ol' throat lump down when offered a first glimpse into the touching realities of personal life for a member of Kiss, when we hear Peter, with a crack in his voice, singing to his wife about how he's unable to join her tonight because he's playing with the band. And our purist protestations aside, how could this song ever have been rendered effectively within the black noise of the usual Kiss sound? No, as hard as it may be to admit, the simple piano, strings, and reeds accompaniment is perfect for the lushly romantic sentiment. Also, for all the complaints about Ezrin's softening the Kiss sound, remember that without him, "Beth" might never have been attempted. Weep, weep.

OK, so "Beth" is too soft for those who want theirs loud, and too light for those who want it hard. Beyond those arguments, "Beth" may have been as important to Kiss's career as "Rock and Roll All Nite." If you don't believe that, keep reading.

Chapter 12
Call of the Wild (Censored)

> We're the partymasters. We lead the party.
> Paul Stanley, October 1976

It would be nearly five months before "Beth" would jump out from behind its veils of orchestration on *Destroyer* and mug the hearts of the parents whose kids had already seen the light of Kiss. In the meantime, a lot of changes went down, not to mention the two and a half singles that were released before the eventual chart triumphs of "Beth."

For starters, Kiss emerged from their hiatus/detour in the studio not only with the *Destroyer* album, but with the Destroyer stage show as well. It was the first major alteration in their concert presentation since they had been launched over two years prior; certainly their nascent superstar status demanded it.

Designed and assembled (to specifications from Kiss and their artistic advisors) by the Broadway stage design firm, Jules Fisher Associates, the new set was more of a play in itself than just a place to play. In keeping with the theme of the album cover, the Destroyer set resembled a huge Gothic city in ruins. To the front of the band, at left and right, were crumbling turrets into which Gene or

Ace could sneak unseen to deliver their solo spots. To the rear of the band was a semidestroyed stone wall (actually constructed of cloth, wood, paint, and papier-mâché) approached by two stairways which the players could mount at selected moments throughout the concert. Set above the wall, after the crew got used to its operation, was a lightning machine that was orginally built for the first *Frankenstein* film in the 1930s. At dramatically opportune moments during the set, the spotlights would dim and this complex contraption would flash into action. On either side of the band there were also gas-powered jets which, likewise, could explode fireballs into the air when the song called for it.

As in the past, Peter was set on an elevator platform, up and to the back of the stage. Much to his relief, the new platform constructed into this set was more spacious than his previous one (of course, now it had to hold two giant papier-mâché mastiffs in addition to drum kit) and, as he pointed out, is "much steadier, though I still nail the drums down," even as it travels a full eight to ten feet higher in the air at the end of the show.

In addition to the stage set, the band donned an entirely refurbished stage wardrobe, corresponding to the album cover: Paul, now bedecked in a sleeker one-piece rhinestone-studded Danskin body suit; Peter, similarly, now in a one-piece with suggestive arrow cut towards the crotch; Ace wearing a lower neckline and higher bootline; and Gene taking on silver plastic armour on his shoulders and incredibly eerie red-eyed gargoyle boots.

Needless to say, when the band headed back

out on that never-ending road after completing recording, audiences, who were larger than ever, were completely amazed. From March to May the revamped and hyperamped Kiss juggernaut crisscrossed the States. In spite of the relative failure of "Shout It Out Loud" and a follow-up single, "Flaming Youth," to carve solid niches in the charts, the LP was selling gangbusters and was assured of moving on from gold to the higher platinum sales award. So with everything in satisfactory order at home, the time had come to take on the rest of the world in earnest.

In June, Kiss and stage set soared off to London, in search of the crack in Britain's indomitable will. And they found it. In a series of near-sold-out shows around England, the outrageous band from the colonies blitzkrieged the populace into submission. It had been expected that, as in America, the press would dismiss the band and its theatrics. It was not expected, however, how thoroughly the fans would embrace them. After two weeks in Merrie Olde, the teen-age subnation was theirs, and, elated, they jetted home as stamped and certified *international* Superstars.

Back in the U.S.A., they are once again Out There, wherever the fans call, on tour, and between frantic nights at packed stadiums and auditoriums, they are keeping busy in their hotel rooms madly scribbling new material for recording, determined to come to the next session completely stocked up.

On July 21, '76, Casablanca puts out a set called *The Originals*, containing the first three LPs and memorabilia. The package becomes a slow but steady seller, eventually chalking up two hundred

and fifty thousand units. But seven days later, on
July 28, Casablanca takes another crack at radio by
releasing a 45 of "Detroit, Rock City."

And that's when it all hits the fan.

On the back side of the single they place Kiss's
second-ever ballad, the only slow song on *Destroyer*,
Peter's "Beth." Then they sit back to wait for the
country to pick up on the wild "A" side, "Detroit," Kiss's latest anthem. But strange things are
happening out in the hinterlands . . .

One day, a deejay somewhere in the middle of
the country (it was never clear where) decides to
check out the flip side to Casablanca's new single.
He slaps it on the turntable and sends it out over
the air. Within a few moments the request phones
in the studio are ablaze with callers. What is that
song? they demand. Play it again. The deejay is
amazed, and suddenly "Beth" is on his playlist.
Ever-alert members of the Kiss Army in the area
take note of the new conquest, and immediately
start planning further invasions. Soon, they are
phoning all the region's radio stations—including
those that devote themselves to Easy Listening
music for oldsters—requesting a song called "Beth"
by a band called Kiss. The Easy Listening program
director is somewhat unsure of who the band is,
but he gives the record a spin. Sure enough, his audience races to their phones to find out more about
that sexy, sad song on the radio. Bingo! Kiss has
landed on the beach of MOR. Within a month, radio programmers across the country are caught up
in the ripple effect of the song's popularity and
"Beth" is Kiss's first major radio smash since

"Rock and Roll All Nite"—and on the soft stations at that.

Soon *all* manner of stations are "on" the record, and by the time the band is ready to head for the studio again, "Beth" has spurred a surge in sales of *Destroyer* that puts the LP millimeters away from the platinum mark—and Kiss into a whole new over-thirty ballpark in addition to the teen-agers.

In September, brimming with new material to work on, and replenished from the unique experience of *Destroyer* and the triumphant British jaunt, Kiss hires out a theater-in-the-round in Nanuet, New York, and calls on Eddie Kramer to produce. Paul delineates what they had in mind: "An excellent classic rock 'n' roll album . . . no strings, no choirs, no keyboards. All guitars. This album is a return to the essence of what Kiss has always gotten off doing. These songs kick ass. They're lethal, heavy-guitar songs. This album I see as the *real* follow-up to *Alive!*" But what about "Beth"? Did he know it would be a hit? Will they perform it on tour? "Yes, next tour. If something's successful, you don't sweep it under the rug. That was not the song I expected to be a hit. And it's not like this album has 'Son of Beth' on it . . ."

Paul goes on to explain that what they are looking for by recording in a theater (with no audience) with the aid of a mobile unit from Electric Lady is a live-in-the-studio sound. "We came here because we wanted to feel more spontaneous. After this we'll never record another album in a studio. There's just too much fire here." And why Eddie Kramer again? "Eddie *is* heavy metal," says Paul.

At the Star Theater, an hour away from the

distractions of New York City, they set up most of
the amps and the drums on the circular stage in the
center of the medium-sized hall with massive
cables running through the vacant audience area to
a dressing roon where Eddie Kramer and the en-
gineer, Corky Stasiak, sat at their consoles. Most of
the basic tracks were played from that stage. The
minimal amount of overdubbing, some guitar solos,
and vocal backups were performed in another
dressing room in front of the theater. The whole
process was not altogether different from the pre-
Echoplex days when singers recorded in tiled
bathrooms in order to get better reverberations of
their voices. In fact, to enhance bass sound on one
song, the band set up Gene's amp way down a long
cinder-block hallway, around which the sounds
bounced back like Superballs.

Ultimately, what came out of all this was *Rock
And Roll Over*, released November 1, 1976. Did
Paul say "fire"? Well, for the first time a Kiss LP
shipped gold, but more importantly, it turned out
to be their rawest, most highly-charged studio set
since the first album. On *Rock And Roll Over*,
Kiss once again responded to the call of the wild.
So obediently and faithfully, in fact, that one of
the country's leading music magazines found it difficult to print a review favorable to the record, as
it conflicted so much with their neoconservative
pose. While Elvis's shaking his hips on the Ed
Sullivan Show is lost to posterity due to archaic
censorship, that *Rock And Roll Over* critique will
not be buried. Rising to the call of the wild, second
hand, I therefore offer here, for the first time, the
Kiss Review They Tried To Murder ʿ(penned as a

lead review by none other than your humble reporter and World's Leading Kiss Authority):

I know. You like Bruce Springsteen, Rod Stewart, Jackson Browne, Stevie Wonder, The Stones, Steely Dan, and, now, Dr. Buzzard's Savannah Band (I knew you'd come around on disco) for the prose-poetry, right? And—correct me if I'm wrong—you get *Playboy* for the articles. Well, I like Kiss for the makeup. And I'm buying this package of rubbers for my father.

The fact of the matter is that, above all, we listen to rock & roll for kicks. Angry, mindless, destructive, offensive, irresponsible kicks. All those things they call sublimated sex. All those things that, sex or no, we still want to do.

Kiss is rock & roll—strictly for kicks. The subject matter of their seven album oeuvre runs the extremely narrow gamut from—to be delicate—money to power to copulation (rarely) to fellatio (as often as possible) to drugs to having a party (pronounced "pawty" and happening much more frequently than birthdays) and most importantly, to rock & roll (a rather nebulous notion generally associated with the aforementioned "pawty"—not to mention drugs, copulation, fellatio, power and money). In other words, it ain't Wittgenstein.

Key song titles illustrating the scope of the oeuvre might include "Makin' Love," "Love 'Em and Leave 'Em," "C'mon and Love Me," and "Calling Dr. Love," as well as "Mainline," "Cold Gin," and, of course, "Rock Bottom," "Detroit, Rock City," "Let Me Go, Rock 'n'

Roll," and Rock and Roll All Nite." The latter
features a line about wanting to play all night
and all day that in its complete implications
may be the summation of the Kiss approach. So,
it ain't Wordsworth either.

But, as they say, it ain't bad rock & roll when
you team it up with its *sine qua non*, a musical
attack (literally) that is, for the most part, unre-
mittingly simple and direct, frequently catchy,
and always counted out on four fingers. And
which is not to be mistaken for the Ramones,
whose primitivism is so blithely arty that it
might have been assembled in a library. While
Kiss is certainly self-conscious, they have never
exhibited the intellectual range to be self-conscious beyond the obvious.

While such a handicap of the vision may not
produce the greatest rock & roll (arguable), it
certainly is great *for* rock & roll. Because with
the ascension of Kiss (and, secondarily, Aerosmith and Ted Nugent), there is hope that the
music may recover from the Great Rock & Roll
Disaster. Namely *Sgt. Pepper's Lonely Hearts
Club Band*, which defused and diffused rock &
roll by presenting in a rock format, alternately, a
bouncy burlesque of the music and pseudo-po-
etic social commentary, all of it thoroughly pal-
atable to Andy Williams and Mick Jagger alike.
At which point Rock became a subset of Pop
and Poetry. Thus, in 1976, on the one hand, the
charts sag under the combined bubble weight of
Peter Frampton and Stevie Wonder. On the
other hand, Led Zeppelin liberally doses us with
Cryptic Messages from the Dark Side of the Cos-

mos (aka Spooky Stories You Tell in the Dark).
And, thus, in '76, an urgent need for Kiss.

   Rock and Roll Over kicks to beat a six-pack
out of Sunday morning. That is: no pop, no
poetry. Smarting from the strictly Platonic
drubbing they took for the schlock-elegant
Destroyer, Kiss has come back with their best,
most consistent album ever. To scrutinize it in
cut-by-cut detail is pointless—essentially redun-
dant if you've read other Kiss reviews. It's
derivative heavy metal rock & roll—derivative,
that is, of everything that has yelped and
screamed and retched molten lava in the past 25
years: Howlin' Wolf, Chuck Berry, the early
Stones, the early Beatles, the Yardbirds, Cream,
the Move, and Free. For the most part, the drums,
as in all of the best rock & roll, do the talking
here. Nearly every song features a crisp open
space where Peter Criss, one of the world's fore-
most two-fisted tom-tom men, lays out the *real*
story in eloquently efficient demolition-style
4/4. Anything else that talks here, you can be
sure, is loud and demonstrative: falling-building
chords, the patented Kiss growl-vocal, and, min-
imally, Ace Frehley's churning and skittering
solo guitar stunts. The lyrics? The usual: *pawty
time!*

   The highlights of this album, which is always
at least good—except for one instance where it is
good but weird—are the Gene Simmons-penned
"Calling Dr. Love" and Paul Stanley's "Mr.
Speed" and "Hard Luck Woman." Sounding like
Mountain's masterpiece, "Mississippi Queen,"
"Dr. Love" opens with what has to be the most

anarchic of the percussionist's weapons, the mighty cowbell, which here sets up a bemusedly bonking counterpoint to some vicious sledgehammer guitar. The song climaxes in a chorus that features a remarkable juxtaposition—and blend—of old and new rock: high and low doo-wop background vocals with a stabbingly syncopated, nastily distorted guitar powerslide. Frehley's solo in "Dr. Love," particularly the reckless bass string fingering that kicks it off, is his best moment of the album. "Mr. Speed," with its near-loping beat and genial Berry-like guitar riff, is almost a change-of-pace for the perennially militant Kiss and definitely the most infectious song here. Paul Stanley's loose and offhand singing is perfect for the teasing Mr. Speed character.

"Hard Luck Woman" is the weird one, mainly because it is the first Perfect Musical Crime. (George Harrison, attention!) Without stepping on copyrights, Kiss pulls off certifiably genuine Rod Stewart, basically "Maggie May," which would be some feat for even the most accomplished rock players. No one has missed a signal: from the melody to the words to the arrangement to—most incredibly—Peter Criss's vocal, the heist is flawless. "Hard Luck Woman" being the album's only near-acoustic and near-slow song, it will undoubtedly function as the follow-up to *Destroyer*'s fluke Easy Listening hit (also sung by Criss), "Beth." And, not to mention, get ol' Rod Stewart running scared.

Which is sort of what I see as the larger function of this band: to get rock & roll running scared. In fact, I hope they stampede all the Pe-

ter Frampton Poppees and the Jackson Browne
Poet People right off the edge of the map. Or
else back around to left field, where rock & roll
started. And they *can* do it as long as they keep
turning out the semiannual hits.

Sure, Kiss is loud. And they've got lyrics so
stupid that the fact that the words are also ridic-
ulously sexist doesn't even count. Their pro-
ductions are generally sloppy and minimal.
They have copped every lick they have, and the
licks that work they recycle endlessly. When in
doubt, their thinking seems to be, play it like a
baseball bat. Plus, they wear this excrutiatingly
comical makeup, which is what I think *really*
scares hell out of the nonbelievers.

All of it is true. Of course. They're a rock &
roll band. And, frankly, I don't love Kiss for
their mind. I love them for their body.

Now, is that really such a disruptive review?
Certainly not. No, what I think really had this
particular magazine so shook up was the album,
not the review. And well they should have been
scared of *Rock and Roll Over*—it's a *killer*!

Chapter 13
It's Reigning Cats &
Bat-Lizards

> What I'd like to know is who the guy is who
> invented the can opener. What an amazing in-
> vention!
>
> Gene Simmons, October 1976

The situation as is stands:

October '76 sees "Beth" still riding high in the
charts and all over the radio, and *Destroyer* is certified by the R.I.A.A. as Kiss's second platinum
record. On October 31, Kiss make their first national network appearance as special guests on *The
Paul Lynde Halloween Special.* On November 1,
Casablanca ships *Rock And Roll Over* to record
stores across the country; it is gold from go.

The situation as it stands: Kiss are top-of-the-
line superstars. And something is missing.

In general, the members of Kiss have to be satisfied that they have fulfilled their lifelong dreams of
stardom out there on the road through America.
But, in specific, there still lies that gnawing need
to come home to the same acclaim, to know that
friends and relatives *see* firsthand that the dream is
now reality. The fact of the matter: Kiss had not
played in New York City proper since the long-
ago Blue Oyster Cult New Year's show at the

Academy. Oh, for sure, they had gained some satisfaction by coming back the following year and topping the bill—but that was out on Long Island. New York City, the five boroughs, that would be the clincher. Then all would know, then *they* would know that those childhood schemes that everybody had taken so lightly were now, in fact, the real thing.

The place to play in New York City when you have made it is Madison Square Garden. On February 18, 1977, Kiss came in off the road, fresh from learning that *Rock and Roll Over* had achieved platinum status, to perform their first concert in Madison Square Garden. And something was no longer missing, the dream complete. Peter Criss told a reporter from the *New York Times* the night before: "I used to tell my folks I'd end up there one day, and they'd always laugh. So tomorrow night we're playing the Garden, and when I think about that I get cold."

Not just *playing* the Garden, but selling out the Garden was the feat Kiss laid out before the Big Apple crowd. Friends, relatives, the press, and thousands of fans all turned out to scream and cheer their heroes, returned home at last. The concert itself was not the slickest show Kiss had ever done, perhaps due to the Garden's impenetrable acoustics and just a little bit of overanxiousness on the band's part, but as far as red-raw emotions went it was the most wide-open, soul-wringing concert anybody has ever put on. After all, for the boys, this was IT!

And what would an Ultimate Conquest be without a victory celebration? Before the last notes of the last encore had time to settle onto the floor of

the arena, we (two of the lucky few) were ex-
citedly on our way to the exclusive Kiss victory
party after the Garden show. When we arrived at
the door of the health club on Manhattan's West
Side, where the bacchanalia was to be held, there
was already a line of frantic well-wishers at the
door ahead of us, all equipped with bathing suits as
our invitation had instructed. Everybody—even the
normally snooty press—wanted to be there to help
Kiss celebrate their new era. Once inside, all par-
tygoers were offered by a toga-outfitted waiter a
scroll on vellum paper neatly tied in a tube with a
ribbon. Unfurling it, one read these words:
"Dream the glory that was Rome. 'The Recovery
of Lost Time' beckons across the years, inviting
you to celebrate a feast to welcome four warriors
home in glorious conquest. The world lies pros-
trate at their feet in adulation. The gods have been
good in bestowing the KISS of success upon our
warriors' brow. Raise your glass—toast their fortune! Fill your plate—taste the morsels dedicated to
their honor." Somehow one gets the feeling there's
something heathen about the whole idea of the
scroll; indeed, something heathen about the
lushness of the party itself! But then . . . It's only
rock 'n' roll—and a helluva lot of fun.

Kiss has not arrived yet, so we take a pair of
sumptuous drinks and head down to the swimming
pool. After a dip in the warm water that seems
such an anomaly after the bitter winter cold outside, we are served another round at poolside by a
Roman waiter with a silver tray, before we travel
back upstairs and to the ballroom teeming with
(oddly enough) disco dancers! We dance, we

drink, and, as advised, taste some of the morsels laid out on three endless banquettes. Scrumptious.

Then the warriors themselves waltz in. All pride aside, the decked-out six-to-sixty crowd of revelers immediately clots around Kiss, and it will be nearly a half hour before the boys can get by the proffered cheeks and hands and slips of paper (for autographs) and drag their other feet in the door of the club. Peter looks very tired. Ace looks his usual spaced-out self. Gene and Paul, on the other hand, are in exuberant spirits, going out of their way to say "hi" to everyone.

Finally, after they've waded through the initial crowd, there is a gap and, set off from the others, there they see what it was all about: their parents. Gene takes the final step of his amazing career, his mother meets him halfway, and they embrace. Paul Stanley and his father step towards one another and shake, both beaming proudly. Kiss has shown *everybody*. They have done what they set out to do, lo, those years ago. They have worked very hard like their parents wanted them to do, and, in the end, it has brought them success, as their parents had said it would—and acceptance by their families as men.

In a moment, Mr. Stanley turns to us and pumps our hands, saying: "Hi, I'm Paul Stanley's father . . . Did you know he can paint too? And very well! I think Kiss is great! I'm very proud. He's a *very* talented boy!"

We know.

Chapter 14
Petit Mort

We're not the same people we were three years ago.

Paul Stanley, October 1976

There is no reason whatsoever for anyone to feel that the rest is anticlimax. Kiss's career reaches new heights every day.

Still, the feeling, a strange regret, a sense of loss, lingers somewhere down in the soul.

What it is, I think, is that February 18, 1977, the Madison Square Garden date, marked the end of a Kiss era—albeit the beginning of a new one, as well. The era that ended was that time in which there was danger for the band. To the day, almost, it marked the end of the first three years since the release of the debut album, and in those three years there were bad times and there were good times. But even when the band was riding high on the crest of two or three platinum albums, somehow one always sensed that they could still fall back, that given some strange and unseen twist of fate, they would *still* lose their fame, their fans, their money. In the first three years they always seemed vulnerable. Perhaps they *were*, and perhaps that's why they tried so goddamned hard, and why they came across to us, their followers, with what

157

all the other groups seemed to lack: a true need for affection, an aching for our Arena Love. In those first three years, then, there always appeared to be something for them to strive for. And something that we could give and take back, if we so pleased (though we gave, we *gave!*). In a way, we and Kiss were partners in the venture for the first three years.

Somehow, though, February 18, 1976 ended all that. Suddenly, Kiss had it all. We remained useful but were no longer *necessary*. And thus, no longer partners. I get the feeling that on February 18, Kiss and Kiss fans sort of went their separate ways (not *too* separate, of course!) and, like old friends breaking up, we were both too sad to shake hands, to acknowledge the new reality. We went back to our seats, and Kiss went back on their stage. I certainly don't believe it was intended to happen this way, but on February 18 I think the time of our innocence ended. Like all children, I thought it would go on forever.

Of course, the Kiss juggernaut has rolled right along and I've sort of gotten used to the whole idea of being a spectator. They're still the greatest band in the land, and, hell, it's sort of nice not to have to worry about them anymore and just be able to sit back (or stand up, more likely!) and enjoy the show. The next show for them was Japan.

Ever since the second album when Kiss printed all the jacket information in Japaneses as well as in English, the Orient has had a dear spot in their hearts for the band, and vice versa. As the years went by, that dear spot got even larger, just as it did here in the States, and currently Kiss is probably the favorite band in Japan. Of course, Kiss and the Japanese were made for each other. First of all, both of them love heavy metal. Secondly, in the Japanese theatre there is a long-standing tradition, called Kabuki, of bizarrely demonstrative white-face makeup that makes the actors look like members of the similarly made-up rock group Kiss.

Suffice it to say that both Kiss and their Oriental fans were primed when the band, accompanied by a slew of junketeering journalists, took off from JFK airport in New York on March 18, destination Tokyo.

One bonus of the Japan tour was that it would be the shakedown cruise for the group's new stage set, the Destroyer staging having been retired shortly after the Garden show (sob). Where the set for Destroyer had been medieval Transylvanian ruins, the new set was futuristic Planet Krypton at the height of its shimmering glory. Their new stage locale is constructed entirely of chrome and clear lucite. Again there is a wall at the rear of the stage, this time of metal, and lucite staircases which are lit from behind when mounted, leading up either side of the drums platform. The drums platform itself is a marvel of the new show; it now has the capability to extend Peter out over the audience as well as up into the air. Combined with the smoke and fire that is always integral to their concert experience, the show is another stunning coup for Kiss.

Though it didn't leave them much time for the healthy tourist pursuits on their first trip to the mysterious East, the band was pleased to learn upon arriving in Japan that all the concerts had completely sold out. That's four cities—Osaka, Nagoya, Fukuoka, and Tokyo—with the four nights they perform in Tokyo's largest venue outgrossing even the Beatles at their peak! Needless to say, the new show went over extremely well in Japan—actually, as long as they were getting their first glimpse of Kiss in person, anything was all right with the fans, a great many of whom turned up in the makeup of their favorite group member, just as at concerts in America. By the time the group departed Japan on April 3, they had a lot more to show from their trip than was evidenced by the bags full of gadgets they toted. Truth to tell, by April 3, Kiss *owned* the whole nation. Like the Americans and English before them, the Japanese too had been conquered by Kiss.

If I've never mentioned a vacation throughout this exegesis, it's because Kiss never seems to take them. But when they got home from Japan, the time was right, and they laid off for nearly six weeks to be with their wives and lovers, write songs, and play with their new cameras and tape decks. Work would be there soon enough: They had booked studio time in the N.Y.C. Record Plant for late May and June. In the interim, *Dressed to Kill* quietly arrived at the gold mark, becoming the band's fourth LP so awarded and the first one of the originals.

Playtime over, the band went into the Record Plant with Eddie "Mr. Heavy Metal" Kramer once again at the knobs, and in quick time they had the desired results: BANG! (as the ads say) *Love Gun*.

It's still difficult to assess the merits of *Love Gun*. Overall, it's a natural follow-up to *Rock And*

Roll Over; it almost sounds like it could have been cut at those same sessions, except that there is something absent. With the exception of the title cut, the songwriting lacks what Paul dubbed "fire" in reference to the previous record. For example, while "Tomorrow and Tonight" is a valiant effort, it's clear that in it Paul is straining much too hard for the past glories of "Flaming Youth" and especially "Rock and Roll All Nite." The song is just not an anthem, and maybe that's not what Paul should be up to at the moment on this particular record. Gene's "Plaster Caster" and "Christine Sixteen" (the latter was the first single) are two songs that certainly fit easily into the sleaze niche of Kiss's recorded works, but even their titles, the easy rhymes, mark them as tunes that may have just been tossed off. In fact, one of the serious structural flaws of *Love Gun* may just be that there is too heavy a load of solo-penned Simmons songs. Had they edited his contributions to the wonderfully disgusting "Almost Human," and had he perhaps collaborated with Paul, who usually has a better melodic sense, this might have been an altogether more satisfying LP. The point about Gene is that he is unbeatable as a creator of lurid atmosphere, but that kind of music is effective only when placed in a context of strong, catchy songs; and Paul's sinisterly triumphant and locomoting "Love Gun" is the sole number that fits that bill.

Love Gun as a restaurant for the ears is long on ambience, short on food. As emphasis of that, the band plays the background vocals heavier on this than on *Rock* and also includes their second oldie, an uneventful, unnecessary remake of the Crystals'

"Then He Kissed Me" (here done from the male point of view). As a sidelight (side dish?) *Love Gun* also contains Ace's first lead-singing stint, on his "Shock Me." The song may not shock, but Ace's pleasant vocalizings are sort of cute.

Of course, one man can spew opinions all day. In the larger scheme it may not matter that the critical jury is still out on this one—at its release on June 30, *Love Gun* was officially the first Kiss album to *ship* platinum (and that means a million units ordered before they even finished recording!). June 30 also represented another red (blood red, in fact) letter day for Kiss and their fans: Stan Lee's Marvel Comics Group published the long-awaited Kiss comic book. In ink partially created from actual blood of Kiss's members, the Marvel gang paints a story about four New York lads who are one day magically transformed into the superheroes Kiss, and wind up tangling with the deadly Dr. Doom. The Kiss comic represents yet another first for the band in that it is the only time Marvel has based a comic on real-life people.

Never content to leave well enough alone, almost the day after their new record and the comic book are released, Kiss heads off for the only place they may ever really feel at home: the road. First a sold-out Canadian tour (their first) with the new set and also new costumes styled to identically match the revamped garb of the *Love Gun* cover, and then, in August, they roll back into the States with the new show honed razor-sharp for the fans that made them in the first place.

Chapter 15

Tomorrow Never Knows

We are younger than any band that's in our class. Everything people are seeing is a band in its infancy. We have not yet peaked, by any means.

Paul Stanley, October 1976

By the time you are reading this, *Alive II* may be available in the stores and the band may be off conquering Outer Mongolia. Another thing they are talking about (or at least Paul is) is the possibility of solo albums in the spring of '78. I wouldn't be surprised. After that I imagine they would be the first rock 'n' roll band to sweep the North and South Poles—*and* get a response from the polar bears! At this point, I can see that overweening Kiss ambition taking the band anywhere, be it on tour or in the studio.

That's the thing: I can't really tell you what's going to be happening to Kiss in the future. I can only tell you that I'm not going to worry about them—they'll always make do—and I can speculate. Here's just a few random events I would like to predict as upcoming for Kiss (and for the rest of rock 'n' roll):

Gene will appear as a character actor in films.

Paul will marry within eighteen months.

Peter and Lydia will have a son within eighteen months.

Gene will write a book that deals heavily with his childhood.

Peter will write one first.

Gene will also script and produce a film with explicit sex scenes.

Paul will play a cameo role in it.

Peter and Lydia will purchase a home near the coast in Massachusetts, where Peter will resume painting seriously.

Ace and Jeanette will purchase a second home in Los Angeles, where he will become involved with session work on his guitar.

Paul's solo album will feature much of his own lead-guitar work, and one of the songs will become a number-one hit single.

Peter will have a one-man exhibition of his paintings at a New York gallery.

Gene's solo album will sell only moderately well, but he will discover and produce a group that will become superstars.

Ace will purchase a private jet.

Paul will continue to live in New York City.

As for the rest of rock 'n' roll:

There will be lots more bands that wear makeup —and all of them will fail miserably.

Chapter 16
Notes of a Kiss Fanatic

Thank God for the rain.
Travis Bickle, May 1976

It's been the hottest July in the city's history, and I haven't gotten up from the desk since the firecrackers. No air conditioning. No air. I guess I *am* working long hours now.

But we go back to the beginning. The first story I ever wrote was about Kiss. Funny, Paul Stanley once told me—I think I mentioned it—he said, "We started to do this because we *believed* in it— not because it was a joke!" And I can say to you now: *I* started to do this because it was a *joke*—not because I was at all serious about it! And now it's been a helluva long time. Years. Further, since September of 1976 it's creeped up to ninety percent of my waking hours—writing about the rock group Kiss, that is. I can hardly believe it. I mean, as of this moment it's been nearly a year without a break.

But I think I did it.

Go ahead. Laugh. I know some of you are wondering how I can face myself in the mornings

165

knowing that yesterday I wrote about Kiss and that today and tomorrow I'm going to do the same. I know that some of you think I'm a jerk or a moron or a fruitcake or whatever people in the outside world—that place beyond the parameters of Kiss—call each other these days. Say what you will: I'm sure I would've felt the same way about someone like myself a few years back. There are others of you, however, who say to me a simple, heartfelt *Right on!* To those I say, Hey, thanks for the support, man, but I don't need it.

But I think I did it.

Because what started out as a joke with me (when I first saw Kiss I thought they were the most ludicrous rip-off to come down the pike in many a moon) (Can you imagine?), and soon thereafter became a hysterical compulsion, then changed again—transubstantiated, I like to think

And I think I did it.

My obsession with Kiss became—and continues to be—none other than an extended journey back and forth through the ages of man. Perfect. And, sure, sometimes it is terrifying, and sometimes it is cruising peacefully in a vaporous blue gyromechanical hum—but, in the final analysis, I think I did it.

I think I became the World's Leading Authority on the rock group Kiss.

Some people in Ohio (I think it was) wrote me a letter and said they would challenge me on that.

But they can't.

They can't hear what's inside of me. They can't know.

If I lift up my ribcage like this and pull it back over my head, can you hear it? Can you hear it now?

(Dumpump-chucka.)

Ohio?

REMISE

Kronology

1945 (ca.)
December 20: Peter Crisscoula (later Criss) born.

1949 (ca.)
August 25: Gene Klein (later Simmons) born.

1950 (ca.)
April 27: Paul (later Ace) Frehley born.

January 20: Stanley Eisen (later Paul Stanley) born.

1970 (ca.)
Gene and Paul come together in same band.

1972 (ca.)
Winter: Gene and Paul derive concept, if not name, for rock group Kiss.

Spring: Gene responds to Peter's ad in *Rolling Stone,* and he and Paul rendezvous with the drummer, who is hired shortly thereafter.

Fall: Gene, Peter, and Paul decide on name Kiss and begin search for lead guitarist. After interminable auditions of incompetents, the three immediately seize on Ace.

1973
January 30: Kiss plays premiere gig at Coventry Club in Queens, New York.

June: Kiss records demo tape at Electric Lady Studios in Manhattan, assisted by friend/producer Eddie Kramer.

July 4: Kiss performs first show at Hotel Diplimat near Times Square in Manhattan.

August 10: Kiss performs second show at Diplomat. Bill Aucoin is in audience and offers band a management deal and a record contract within two weeks.

August 24: Kiss signs as first act with Neil Bogart's fledgling Casablanca Records.

October: Kiss records debut album, *Kiss,* at Bell Sound Studios in Manhattan.

1974
February 8: *Kiss* is released.

May: On tour in San Francisco, Paul receives rose tattoo on shoulder from Lyle Tuttle.

August-September: Kiss records second LP, at Village Recorder in Los Angles.

October 22: *Hotter Than Hell* is released.

December 31: Kiss opens for the Stooges and Blue Oyster Cult at New Year's Eve heavy-metal spectacular at the Academy of Music on Fourteenth Street in New York City. Gene ignites hair during performance.

1975
January 10: "Let Me Go, Rock 'n' Roll," first *official* single from Kiss, is released.

February: Kiss records third LP, again at Village Recorders in LA: Neil Bogart produces.

March 19: *Dressed To Kill* is released.

April 2: "Rock And Roll All Nite" released as a single.

June: Kiss sells out Cobo Hall concert in Detroit. Eddie Kramer tapes show.

July 10: "C'mon And Love Me" released as single.

September 10: *Kiss Alive!,* their fourth LP, is released.

October 14: Live "Rock And Roll All Nite" is released as single and becomes band's first big hit.

November: *Alive!* becomes Kiss's first gold LP, as certified by R.I.A.A.

December: Kiss begins recording fifth album, at Record Plant in Manhattan with Bob Ezrin producing.

December 31: Blue Oyster Cult opens for Kiss at Nassau County Veteran's Coliseum on Long Island.

1976
January: *Alive!* certified platinum by the R.I.A.A.

February 15: *Creem* Magazine publishes first major Kiss article by the self-proclaimed World's Leading Authority on Rock Group Kiss.

March 1: Preview single, "Shout It Out Loud," from new LP is released.

March 15: *Destroyer,* sixth Kiss LP, is released.

April: *Destroyer* certified gold. Destroyer tour with new set begins.

April 30: "Flaming Youth" single is released.

June: Kiss embarks on first British tour.

July 21: *The Originals,* a three-record compilation package, is released.

July 28: Single version of "Detroit, Rock City" is released; flip side: "Beth."

August: "Beth" climbs into charts.

September: Kiss begins recording new LP live-in-the-studio at the Star Theater in Nanuet, New York; Eddie Kramer producing. "Beth" becomes bona fide hit single. *Destroyer* is certified as Kiss's second platinum album.

October 31. Kiss performs first national TV appearances on *The Paul Lynde Halloween Special.*

November 1: *Rock And Roll Over* is released, first Kiss album to "ship" gold.

December 1: "Hard Luck Woman" is released as single.

1977
January: *Rock And Roll Over* certified platinum.

February 18: Kiss performs triumphant homecoming concert in New York City's Madison Square Garden.

March 18: Kiss departs for first tour of Japan with new stage set.

April 3: Kiss returns from Japan, begins first vacation.

May-June: Kiss records again at Manhattan's Record Plant with Eddie Kramer.

June 30: *Love Gun* is released, "ships" platinum (first Kiss LP to do so).

July 1: Kiss embarks on first official Canadian tour with new costumes and new Love Gun set.

August: Kiss swings south to U.S. for American debut of Love Gun tour.

November-December: *Alive II* "ships" platinum.

1978
February-March: Kiss begins pre-production work on TV and film projects in Los Angeles.

April: Gene linked with Cher in *People* magazine cover story.

May: Solo LPs in the offing?

May: Double platinum released, "ships" platinum cimpilation album of old cuts.

May: Gene Simmons and Cher Allman rumoured engagement.

September: Each member releases solo album. All four "ship" double platinum.

1979
June: *Dynasty*, "ships" platinum. Top 10 hit in U.K. with "I was Made for Loving You".

1980
Double album move soundtrack (projected).

March: Savoy Books release *Kiss* by Robert Duncan.

2001
June: Kiss releases 36th album, 16th video disk.

A Quick Incomplete Guide to Some Kiss Bootlegs

1976
Kiss live at the Free Trade Hall, Manchester
Deuce
Strutter
100,00 Years
Very poor quality

Kiss Blitz, London. Recorded at the Hammersmith Odeon
Deuce
Strutter

Kiss, Cleveland, Ohio
Deuce
Strutter
Fire House

1977
Second Kiss
Deuce
Strutter
Detroit Rock City
Fair Quality

Kiss tapes, Tokyo
Detroit Rock City
Take Me
Cold Gin (full)
God of Thunder (with bass solo)
Approx length 1 hr.

Kiss live at the L.A. Forum
God of Thunder
Shock Me (full)
Bad quality

Kiss Destroys Anahiem Pts 1 & 2. Recorded at the concert where
Kiss blew up the Destroyer set.
Deuce
God of Thunder
Detroit Rock City

Kiss My Axe
Take Me
I Stole Your Love
Shock Me
Bad Quality

1977-78
Sneak Attack, Long Island
I Stole Your Love
God of Thunder
Good quality

1979
Kiss live (at Maddison Square Gardens?)
I was Made for Loving You
Move On
New York Groove
2,000 Man

Kiss (Kapon) Tapes
Collection Of, Best Cuts Of, Tapes Tokyo, Anahiem and LA
Forum.